.3

AYLESBURY
A History

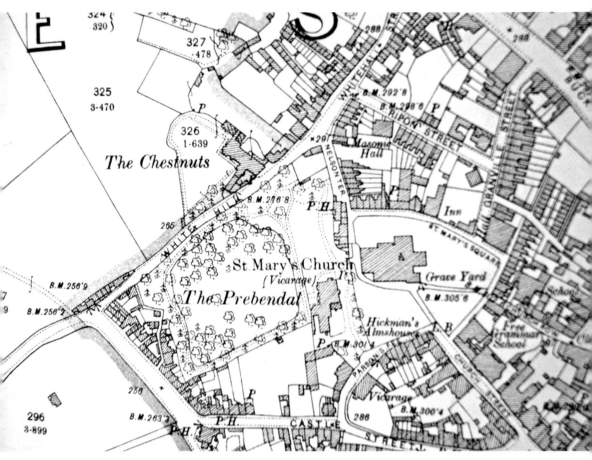

The churchyard area in 1898 showing new streets to the north.

AYLESBURY

A History

HUGH HANLEY

PHILLIMORE

2009

Published by
PHILLIMORE & CO. LTD
Chichester, West Sussex, England
www.phillimore.co.uk
www.thehistorypress.co.uk

© Hugh Hanley, 2009

ISBN 978-1-86077-496-6

Printed and bound in Great Britain

Contents

LIST OF ILLUSTRATIONS

Frontispiece: The churchyard area in 1898 showing new streets to the north

ACKNOWLEDGEMENTS

I have had generous assistance in producing this book, not least in relation to the illustrations. I am particularly indebted to Roger Bettridge, County Archivist, and the staff of the Centre for Buckinghamshire Studies, to Brett Thorne of the County Museum Service and to Diana Gulland, Honorary Archivist and Librarian to the Buckinghamshire Archaeological Society. Special thanks are also due to Michael Farley, Hon. Deputy Editor of *Records of Buckinghamshire*, the journal of the Buckinghamshire Archaeological Society, for sharing his unrivalled knowledge of the town's prehistory, to Eric Throssell for lending illustrations and for helpful information and suggestions, to the invaluable assistance of Roger King of the Aylesbury Society in taking and collating all the photographs and to Aylesbury town council for the use of their office facilities. Father Shane Woods, Vicar of Aylesbury, kindly facilitated access to monuments in the parish church of St Mary's. John Kirwan in distant Kilkenny kindly supplied photographs of monuments at Gowran (24) and Anna Eavis of the National Monuments Record Centre was most helpful in arranging permission to use items subject to Crown copyright.

Acknowledgement is made to the following for access to and/or permission to reproduce illustrations in their possession: The Centre for Buckinghamshire Studies for the following: 13 (ref. BAS/E189/48), 33 (BAS/E198/48), 37 (BAS/E199/48), 38 (AR/6/89), 39 (AR16/89), 40 (PR11/1/1), 49 (D/X 1007/48/1), 50 (PR11/12 /1), 57 (N/Q/1/6/1), 59 (D/X 801/20/2), 60 (L/Md/1/8), 62 (D/X801/9), 66 (D/LE/H/12), 70 (BAS/173/47), 72 (D15/1/2), 80 (D15/1/2), 71 and 83 (D/LE/H/12), 73 and 88 (Q/RSf/5), 90 (BAS101/4), 102 (D/X702/2), 103 (D/X702/1), 92-3, 96-9 and 107 (D15/1/2), 105 (news cuttings, 372:38), 100 and 110 (PHX 2/1), 122, 123-9 (PHX 214/1), 130 (directory); The Buckinghamshire County Museum, 1, 9, 11, 25, 30-2, 44-5, 48, 67-9, 74, 79, 104, 120-1, 134, 136. The County Archaeological Service, 2, 6. The Buckinghamshire Archaeological Society, 46-7, 61, 76, 78, 81-2, 91, 95, 101, 109, 112, 117, 119. The Aylesbury Society, 4, 15, 28, 53, 58, 67, 69, 111-12, 113-14, 131, 135, 137, 141, 143, 146, 149. Aylesbury Town Council, 17-18, 27, 34, 42, 63-4, 112, 113, 114, 138, 144-5. Aylesbury Vale District Council, 139, 150. The National Trust, 29. English Heritage, 123-9 (CBS PHX214/1). Dept of the Environment, Heritage and Local Govt, Dublin, 23. Michael Farley, 7-8, 10. Roger King, 26, 87, 133, 146. Eric Throssell, 22, 51, 86.

Author's royalties have been gifted to The Aylesbury Society.

One

URBAN ORIGINS

Aylesbury lies close to the meeting place of Buckinghamshire's two principal contrasting landscapes. To the north is the clay Vale to which it gives its name, with its gentle rolling fields and nucleated villages, and to the south the chalk hills of the Chilterns, famed for their beech woods and associated historically with much more dispersed forms of settlement. The old town is situated on a low limestone hill, an island in a sea of heavy clay, encircled on three sides by the flood plain of the river Thame, a tributary of the Thames, and its meandering tributary streams. These streams define the ancient boundary with neighbouring parishes on the north and west and also with the hamlet of Walton in Aylesbury, situated on another Portland ridge less than half a mile south of the town centre. A few miles to the north in earlier times lay the great forest of Bernwood extending westwards into Oxfordshire. Aylesbury is also at the centre of a network of roads, large and small, which radiate out in all directions. Historically, the most important of these is the Akeman Street (now the A41), the Roman road linking *Verulamium* (St Albans) to Cirencester and Bath and connecting to the Icknield Way, the prehistoric trackway from Wessex to East Anglia, which runs along the scarp of the Chiltern hills.

Recent archaeological investigations at the Prebendal House have revealed that Aylesbury's first settled inhabitants were Iron-Age Celts, who in the fifth century B.C. chose the commanding hilltop location as a suitable site on which to erect a hill fort consisting of a deep ditch surrounded by an earthen mound enclosing an area of some eight hectares, including the inner core area of the medieval town but excluding the present market place. Buried within the ditch was a severed head, a deliberate deposit packed around with limestone blocks, while inside the fort were found parts of at least five human bodies and the remains

1   *Neolithic flint axehead*
    (c.3000-4,000 B.C.).

1

2 *Excavation of a portion of an Iron-Age hillfort's ditch at the Prebendal House in 1985.*

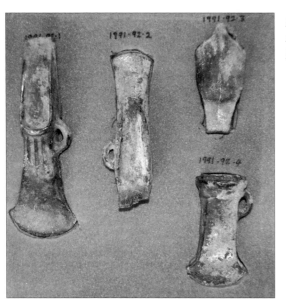

3 *Late Bronze-Age axeheads, or looped palstaves, 2,600-2,800 years old. A hoard found at Manor Drive, Aylesbury.*

ERECTED BY THE AYLESBURY SOCIETY

IN 1973
DEMOLITION OF A
TUDOR BUILDING ON THIS
SITE EXPOSED AN INFILLED
DITCH 9 FEET DEEP WHICH ONCE
FORMED PART OF THE
TOWNS DEFENCES.

FOR EUROPEAN HERITAGE DAYS 1993

4 *Plaque on Bourbon Street.*

5 *Another section of the Iron-Age ditch revealed by the demolition of old houses in Kingsbury in 1999.*

6 *A severed head. The careful positioning of this skull found at the bottom of the ditch, the nature of the cut and the presence of other human and animal remains testify to deliberate slaughter. Similar evidence of ritual foundation sacrifice has been found at other hillfort sites.*

of at least thirty beasts, unique evidence of a gruesome foundation ritual. Within a century or so the site was abruptly abandoned by its inhabitants and it lay deserted for over a millennium, a place used only for the grazing of sheep and cattle until the ditch was re-cut in the Middle Saxon period. It is this landmark which is commemorated in the place-name Aylesbury (Aegelesburh), the burh or fort of Aegel. Aegel's identity is uncertain but a possible candidate is Aegil, the sun-archer demi-god of Anglo-Saxon mythology, brother to the better known Weland the Smith.

Meanwhile successive waves of settlers – Bronze-Age Celts, Romans and Saxons – had left their marks on the surrounding landscape. The Celts favoured the light soils of the Chilterns, as did the Romans, whose principal urban centre in the region was at *Verulamium* (St Albans). The Romans converted the prehistoric Akeman Street track into a paved highway and established a small military fort, one of a chain of such roadside defences, at nearby Fleet Marston and also possibly at Walton. Archaeological evidence shows that Roman villas and other domestic dwellings, though not numerous, were quite widely distributed in the immediate area, testimony to a state of relative peace and tranquillity.

The situation altered with the recall of the legions in A.D. 407 and the arrival of Germanic tribesmen, first as auxiliary soldiers, then in greater numbers as settlers living alongside the Romano-British inhabitants, and eventually as rivals and supplanters, though a degree of gradual peaceful assimilation has to be presumed. Sunken round houses and other evidence of Saxon settlement excavated at Walton in the 1970s have been dated to the late fifth century and it has been suggested

7 Burials in Aylesbury plotted on an OS map of 1884. Multiple burials are indicated by a solid black circle; a single or unknown number by a partially solid circle. Known burial grounds are shaded dots.

8 The same map with conjectured approximate line of hillfort ditch added.

that the settlement may have originated as a base for auxiliary cavalry guarding the Akeman Street route. This formative, but obscure, period also saw the emergence of tribal groupings led by rival chieftains, but the process of settlement was for the most part a very gradual one, especially in the Chilterns where the assimilation of the indigenous British population was spread over several centuries.

The first written reference to Aylesbury by name is in the Anglo-Saxon Chronicle in a much disputed and almost certainly retrospective entry under the year 571, in which Aylesbury is included among the four 'towns' (the others were Limbury, Bensington and Eynsham) said to have been captured from the 'Britons' by a West-Saxon ruler called Cuthwulf. But since we now know that in 571 Aylesbury

9 *Small Roman jar from a railway cutting at Haydon Hill, Aylesbury.*

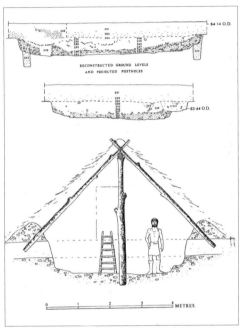

10 *Artist's impression of 'sunken'-type Saxon house from the settlement at Walton Court excavated in 1973-4.*

was merely the site of an imposing earth-work, this story must be regarded as at best misleading. The evidence suggests that the beginnings of continuous, permanent settlement at Aylesbury came later and that they are associated with two simultane-ous developments which occurred in the late seventh century: the conversion of the Anglo-Saxons, which was almost complete by A.D. 700, and the expansion of the king-dom of Mercia from its centre in the Trent valley as far south as the upper Thames, thus bringing the area inhabited by the Cil-ternsaete, the 'dwellers by the Chilterns'

referred to in the late seventh-century doc-ument known as the Tribal Hidage, within its ambit. The Mercian hegemony lasted until the rise of the kingdom of Wessex in the mid-ninth century.

What we can say with a degree of confidence is that at some date in the late seventh century, and certainly before 710-20 at the latest, the ditch of the Iron-Age hill fort was re-cut, in part at least on the same alignment, to a depth of nearly two metres and that this enclosure became the site of an important early minster, a monastic settlement of a peculiarly English type.

Such re-use of ancient hill forts for religious purposes was by no means uncommon and there are at least three other later examples in Buckinghamshire, and in other respects too the location was eminently suitable. Excavations of burials at George Street have confirmed other evidence for an extensive minster churchyard dating from the early ninth to the early 10th centuries. The popularity of the minster as a burial place is in itself a convincing guarantee of its mother status.

It was during the reigns of King Wulfhere (657-75) and his brother Ethelred (675-704), the Christian sons of the redoubtable pagan Penda (d. 655) of Mercia, when new dioceses were being established to serve the Anglo-Saxon kingdoms, that a sustained effort was made to establish Christianity in the southern territories of the Mercians. A major element in this process was the foundation of minsters, an activity in which noble ladies of the royal house of Mercia were heavily involved. Two of the five daughters of Penda seem to have become nuns and abbesses of minsters founded by their brother Wulfhere, probably in the period 660-5. They were Eadburgh, who appears from a later tradition to have ruled a minster at Bicester, and Eadgyth (Edith), presumed to be the abbess at Aylesbury of that name who figures in the legend of Aylesbury's patron saint Osgyth, better known as Osyth. These establishments were probably double houses, made up of both men and women under the rule of an abbess.

According to her legend, preserved in 12th-century sources, Osyth was the daughter of a king, Fredeswald, and his wife Wilburh, yet another sister of Wulfhere. She is said to have been born in her father's palace at Quarrendon and brought up in her aunt's nunnery at Aylesbury. Fredeswald is probably Frithuwold, the Mercian sub-king who in 672/4, in an extant charter confirmed by Wulfhere at his residence at Thame, Oxfordshire, endowed Chertsey minster in Surrey. Such sub-kings were a feature of Mercian rule. At the age of 13 Osyth was married to Sighere, a ruler of the East Saxons. With her husband's acquiescence she eventually took the veil and founded a minster at Chich (now St Osyths) in Essex. She is said to have been killed by pirates and buried at Chich. There is evidence to suggest that her body was later removed to Aylesbury, presumably for greater safety during the Danish invasions, where, according to the antiquary Leland, it remained for 46 years before being returned to Chich. In the 15th century Chich successfully opposed Aylesbury's claim to possess the rediscovered relics of St Osyth.

Since the principal purpose of early minsters was to evangelise the indigenous population within an area of 10 to 15 miles or more, the presence of priests can be assumed. There would also have been a church – sometimes more than one – within the precinct. In 1978 traces of a possible late Saxon tower were found under the west end of the nave of the present parish church of Saint Mary's, and Gibbs in his history of Aylesbury refers to a supposed Saxon arch in the crypt, now built up, but these, if correct, evidently do not relate to the earliest phase of building.

Minsters, and especially royal foundations, could expect to receive endowments for the upkeep of the community. These would have taken the form of gifts of land, usually secured by a written charter, or 'land book', embodying a new concept of proprietary landholding introduced by the Church into a society in which lordship rather than ownership was the norm, acknowledged in the form of food renders. Aylesbury minster was no exception, for

Domesday Book (1086) tells us that the then manor of Stoke (Mandeville) 'lies with the [lands of] Aylesbury church'. Uniquely, however, the same entry goes on to tell us that each freeman in the eight hundreds 'which lie in the circuit of Aylesbury' who has one hide (an amount of land for the support of one free family, usually estimated at around 120 acres) or more of land owes one load of corn to this church and that prior to 1066 each freeman had paid an acre of corn or 4d. Here is further confirmation of Aylesbury's antiquity and local primacy because this form of contribution, known as church scot, which was to be gradually superseded by tithe, was an entitlement.

Clues to the location of the lands belonging to Aylesbury minster can also be found in local place names. Buckland ('book land'), the name of a nearby parish, denoting as it does land given to the church, is an obvious example. Stoke (Old English *stoc*), as in Stoke Mandeville, can have the meaning 'a religious place, a secondary settlement'. Walton, a settlement within the parish of Aylesbury, and Caldecote, a 'lost' settlement which was at least partly situated in Aylesbury, are both names which are widely associated with early minsters. Cot villages (there are also villages called Hulcott and Burcott immediately to the east of Aylesbury) were also low-status places inhabited by smallholders called cottars or bordars. It is now thought that some cot names could belong to the period before 850 and a significant minority can be associated with nascent urban settlements. Minsters were useful to rulers – themselves peripatetic – both as sources of hospitality and as centres of administration.

The late seventh century, which saw the foundation of Aylesbury's minster, also saw increasing Saxon penetration of the Chiltern hills for woodland and grazing as well as permanent settlement. Aylesbury gave its name to one of the territorial divisions called hundreds which extended from Aylesbury and Bierton in the Vale south to Wendover and Great Hampden in the Chilterns. Though the formal use of the term dates from the ninth and tenth centuries, it has been shown that many hundreds had their origins in earlier land units. When the hundreds were grouped together early in the 11th century Aylesbury became the head of a triple hundredal unit comprising Aylesbury, Stone and Risborough hundreds – the so-called three hundreds of Aylesbury. But, long before this, Buckinghamshire had come into existence as a new, artificial, administrative unit, formed from an amalgamation of pre-existing hundreds in order to provide support for the new defended burh, or fortress, founded by Edward the elder at Buckingham in 911, as one in a chain of such defences forming part of his strategy for the re-conquest of the Danelaw. The creation of this planned proto-urban settlement with its distinctive status would be the source of future rivalries for primacy within the new shire.

It seems unlikely that Aylesbury itself escaped completely unscathed during the Danish invasions, which began in the ninth century. In the year 917, for example, the Anglo-Saxon Chronicle tells us that a Danish army was raiding between Bernwood Forest and Aylesbury. But, like the majority of minster sites, Aylesbury retained its local saint and its burial functions, indicating that it must have been an important site throughout, though by this time double minsters (i.e. male and female) with their strong monastic ethos had been replaced at local level by priests, who in some places appear to have been formally organised in colleges.

From the ninth and 10th centuries, a period in which more settled local communities and a communal form of agriculture were emerging in the Vale of Aylesbury, rulers were increasingly bolstering their power by establishing bases close to minsters. The place-name Kingsbury, found in proximity to a minster site, as at Aylesbury, can have this implication. Aristocrats, too, exploited minsters in this way. In around 971 Ealdorman Aelfheah of Hampshire, 'one of the small group through whom Edgar governed England', bequeathed lands at Aylesbury as well as at several other minster places to the king. How Aelfheah had acquired the land in the first place is not known (probably from the king), nor is it often clear to what extent, if at all, in this period a particular minster actually benefited from the endowments which nominally belonged to it.

An important demonstration of the royal authority at this time was the establishment of royal mints locally, in part as a result of King Edgar's great re-coinage of 973. The Aylesbury mint is one of only two which are definitely known to have existed in the county (the other was in Buckingham). The names of eight of the moneyers have been preserved on coins dating from the reign of Aethelred (968-1016) to Harold (d.1066). The mint is probably commemorated by the now vanished Silver Street, as the association of the name with former mint towns has been noted elsewhere. In the laws of Athelstan (924-39) it had been decreed that 'there shall be no minting except in a port', a word meaning a town or market town as distinct from a fortified burh. It is thus reasonable to conclude that Aylesbury already had a market of sorts by the 970s. The reason for the diversion of the Roman road at Walton to enter Aylesbury by the present Walton Street, which also occurred in the 10th century, is uncertain but is likely to be connected in some way with the settlement at Walton. Certainly the low-lying Walton Street section of the diversion can hardly have been much of an improvement, judging by later complaints about its condition. The original route was only restored with the adoption of the present High Street in 1826.

Less than twenty years before the Norman Conquest, King Edward the Confessor, who was probably no stranger to Aylesbury since he had built himself a hunting lodge at nearby Brill, bestowed the church of Aylesbury, together with those of Buckingham and of Leighton Buzzard in Bedfordshire, on Bishop Wulfwig, whom he had appointed to the see of Dorchester-on-Thames in 1053. By 1086 William the Conqueror had transferred these endowments to the newly created see of Lincoln. Meanwhile the fragmentation of the old multiple estates continued. The ancient parish of Aylesbury, comprising the manors

11a and b   *Rare Anglo-Saxon silver penny of Edward the Confessor (1042-66), minted at Aylesbury. The names of eight Aylesbury moneyers have been preserved. (Left, obverse; right, reverse).*

of Aylesbury and Walton, occupied an area of some 3,000 acres, of which the hamlet and manor of Walton accounted for more than a third. The manor of Aylesbury (more accurately Aylesbury-with-Bierton) also included a sizeable area of Bierton (the parish boundary itself was not finalised until the 13th century and it left some enclaves of Bierton within Aylesbury parish). The parish boundaries with Bierton on the north-east and with Stoke Mandeville and Weston Turville on the south-east have for most of their length the straight-edged indentations characteristic of open-field furlongs, evidence that this form of communal agriculture was already in use when they were laid out, probably in the late Anglo-Saxon period.

In Domesday Book, where Aylesbury appears first under the heading of 'Land of the King', we are simply told that 'The Bishop of Lincoln holds the church of this manor.' Of Stoke (Mandeville), which is included among the Bishop of Lincoln's lands, it is stated, 'This manor lies with [the lands of] Aylesbury Church' and that Bishop Wulfwig held it with the church before 1066. There follows the information about the tribute due to Aylesbury church to which reference has previously been made.

This is not the whole story of the church's endowments, however, for in his charter of 1090 confirming his father's gifts to the new cathedral of Lincoln William II refers to 'the church of Aylesbury with lands and tithes, namely Stoke Mandeville, Walton and Buckland'. Walton, though nowhere mentioned in Domesday, was as we have seen part of Aylesbury and moreover a manor belonging to Aylesbury church, while Buckland belonged to the Bishop of Lincoln. In 1066 it had been held by Wulfwig's brother Godric, who could not grant or sell it without his permission, an arrangement which smacks of nepotism. Domesday Book thus confirms Aylesbury's status as a primary mother church. But whereas some ancient minsters succeeded in transforming themselves into collegiate churches, Aylesbury had lost whatever independence it had previously possessed by the transfer of its endowments to the control of the bishop. Henceforth these endowments would be used for the support of various members of the cathedral chapter at distant Lincoln (they were usually leased to local tenants).

More generally, from as early as the mid-10th century the position of minsters was being undermined by the emergence of a growing network of private, one-priest, parish churches. Local lords played a leading role in this. Under legislation of King Edgar a thegn could claim the right to endow a church having a graveyard with a third of his demesne tithes. In Domesday Book only four churches (Aylesbury, Haddenham, North Crawley and Buckingham) are mentioned by name, but we know of at least one other, Whitchurch, which on the evidence of its name (white church) was in existence in 1086, and All Saints, Wing, can be assigned on architectural grounds to the seventh-eighth centuries. There were probably others and the following century would reveal the existence of many more recent foundations.

In the process it was inevitable that the ancient minster churches should suffer a diminution of their status. Around the year 1140, for example, Robert de Tenchebrai, a local lord, granted half a hide of land in Quarrendon, with the whole tithe of his demesne and of his men, to the church of Saint Mary of Aylesbury in exchange for the grant of the right to have a cemetery at Quarrendon. As one historian puts it, 'Burial at a minster, once a privilege, had become a nuisance.' Quarrendon, Bierton,

Buckland and Stoke Mandeville, all now appropriated to Lincoln, became chapels of Aylesbury in this period but were later separated from it.

But if its importance as a local religious centre was declining, Aylesbury's secular importance as a town on the royal demesne was not. Buckingham, as the shire's only borough (*burgus*), has pride of place at the head of the Buckinghamshire Domesday record. Here some 27 tenants, styled 'burgesses', owing money rents to various lords also owed payments to the king. Although it had virtually lost its original function as a fortress, it retained the legal and other attributes of a royal borough. But Aylesbury was clearly the more prosperous place. It was unique in the county in possessing tolls, from which it paid £10, a very large sum which is evidence of the existence of a flourishing market there in 1086. Notable also is the amount of its 'farm', the annual payment due to the crown which, at £56, in addition to the toll, is the largest for any Buckinghamshire

manor and more than twice that paid by Buckingham. Even more remarkably, the farm had more than doubled in value since 1066. A reference to a freeman holding a virgate (a unit of roughly thirty acres) of land there, 'who always follows the king's sheriff', may also be significant insofar as it seems to confirm the town's role as a centre for royal administration.

In other respects Aylesbury does not differ markedly from other large rural manors and seemingly justifies F.M. Stenton's inclusion of it among those trading places where 'the trading community must have been a mere appendage to a royal manor'. The vill answers for 16 hides (the demesne is not separately assessed to hides). The land is described as sufficient for 16 ploughs, two of which are in lordship, with four more possible. Two mills are valued at 23s. and there is meadow enough for eight ploughs, a plentiful supply, reflecting the extent of the flood plain (neighbouring Quarrendon, a much smaller parish, but closer to the river, has meadow for 10 ploughs). There is no mention of pasture or woodland.

However, the number of recorded tenants of the manor is suspiciously low, as well as of low status, comprising as it does just 20 villeins, or villagers, 14 bordars, or smallholders (we are told that there could be four more), and two slaves, together with the freeman previously mentioned – a total of well under fifty. Yet not only was Aylesbury a trading centre, it was also a large agricultural unit. The most likely explanation for this apparent discrepancy is that both the precinct of the minster, an area in the centre of the town which could have been encroached upon by traders, and the Lincoln manor of Walton, which is not mentioned by name in Domesday Book, have for some unknown reason been omitted.

TERRA REGIS.

Eilesberia dñicū maneriū regis. p̄ xvi. hid̄ fe defd̄ sēp. Tra. ē. xvi. car̄. In dñio funt. ii. Ibi xx. uilli cū. xiiii. bord. hñt. x. car̄. 7 adhuc. iiii. poſ fieri. Ibi. ii. ſerui. 7 ii. molini de. xxiii. ſol. Ptū. viii. car̄. 7 de remanenti. xx. ſol. In totis ualentijs reddit. lvi. lib̄ arſas 7 penſatas. 7 de Theloneo. x. lib̄ ad numerū. T.R.E. reddeb̄ xxv. lib̄ ad numerū In hoc m̄ fuit 7 eſt. unus ſochs habeſ. i. uirḡ træ quā potuit dare l̄ uende cui uoluit. 7 tam ſeruit sēp uicecomiti regis. Æcclam huj m̄ ten̄ eps̄ Lincolienſis.

12   Aylesbury's entry in the Domesday Book of 1086, which comes first in the category of King's Land (Terra Regis), makes clear its importance, owing as it did the very large annual payment of £56 as well as £10 from tolls. Elsewhere in Domesday there evidence of the antiquity and 'mother' status of its church.

Two

FEUDAL AYLESBURY: A ROYAL MANOR

After the Conquest Aylesbury remained a royal manor throughout the whole of the 12th century until 1204, when it was granted by King John to his justiciar, or chief minister, Geoffrey fitz Peter, created Earl of Essex in 1199, whose descendants, the Mandevilles, held it for most of the following century by the service of one knight's fee and an annual 'farm', or rent of £60 (£4 more than in 1086). This period saw significant change and growth, in the course of which the town's status as the principal seat of royal administration and justice within the shire was confirmed and expanded.

There is some evidence for the erection of a castle, possibly a product of the civil unrest that marked the reign of Stephen (1135-54). Today no trace of the castle survives but remains of what was taken to be such were still visible above ground as late as the 18th century, when a visitor describes it as situated on the west side of the town. It seems to have been a small, and probably relatively short-lived, structure of the motte and bailey type, of which examples survive at High Wycombe and nearer home at Weston Turville and Wing.

Manors such as Aylesbury forming part of the royal demesne had a number of distinguishing features which had long-term tenurial implications. Villeins, or bondsmen, on the king's demesne, though technically unfree, came to enjoy privileges denied to bondsmen on other estates. The terms on which they held their lands were in general comparatively light and, crucially, they came to acquire a special right of access to the king's courts which was denied to villeins elsewhere. In return they were liable – as were inhabitants of boroughs – to an arbitrary royal tax called tallage. Henry II (1154-89) appears to have believed in encouraging his villeins to prosper so that he could tallage them more effectively, unlike lesser lords who tended to squeeze as much as they could from their tenants in rents, dues and services.

Even when a royal manor was granted away, as happened with Aylesbury in 1204, tenants on 'ancient demesne of the crown' retained their former privileges and Aylesbury's manorial tenants were still claiming the status at least as late as the 16th century. Henry II actively promoted the growth of towns and trade, though he was reluctant to grant them too much independence. Another nearby town, Dunstable in Hertfordshire, owed its existence to one of his recent predecessors, Henry I (1100-35), who built a royal residence there known later as Kingsbury.

Aylesbury's connection with the monarch prior to 1204 was more than purely formal, for kings in this period were still peripatetic, constantly on the move from one royal manor house to another, usually with a large escort, consuming stored-up provisions as they went. Aylesbury was close to the royal hunting lodge at Brill within the forest of Bernwood, which itself lay on the route from Windsor to the royal residence at Woodstock, and both Henry I and Henry II are known to have visited at least once. The royal manor house, or 'hospice' (*hospitium*), together with the manorial outbuildings and barns, would probably have been situated in, or near, the present Kingsbury (king's burh, or fort). Together with the extensive precinct of the ancient minster, Aylesbury's Kingsbury was one of the core elements in the emerging urban settlement (at this period the market is likely to have been located close to the church).

A written survey, made following the accession of Henry II in 1154, assesses the stock and produce on the demesne, or home farm, of the manor of Aylesbury. There was a variety of livestock including 30 oxen (for ploughing), 28 swine, 24 pigs, 457 sheep, a piggery, four cattle sheds and three carts. The bulk of the unthreshed grain, harvested in the great open fields of the manor, was stored in two large aisled barns. One of the barns was full of wheat and the other contained oats and there were in addition stacks of oats and wheat and a heap of threshed oats. No other crops are mentioned. The manor as a whole is stated in the survey to have been worth £50 in the reign of Henry I, i.e. before the civil wars of Stephen's reign, £6 less than in 1086. It was a large establishment by the standards of the time, when grain yields were much smaller than today. It was also considerably larger than that of

the royal manor at Brill, surveyed at the same time, which had one barn, not full, and much less livestock. The names of the five jurors who attested the survey are a mixture of Norman and English. They are Ralf, Blakeman, Adwi, Walter son of Tovi and Richard of Burcott.

According to sworn inquests taken in the late 14th century the hospitals of St Leonard and St John the Baptist were founded by certain men of Aylesbury, with the support and confirmation of Henry I and Henry II, for the benefit of lepers and of infirm and impoverished inhabitants of Aylesbury respectively. St Leonard's, the leper hospital, was founded by Samson son of William, Reginald Wauncy, William son of Aldvy (one version has Alan) and others not named, and St John's was founded by Robert Hale (or atte Hide), William son of Richard (or Robert), William atte Hide, John Palkok and others. The inhabitants of Aylesbury who had thus united in a form of corporate enterprise not normally found outside towns in this period were not knights or landowners but probably belonged to a community which existed in part by trade. That their names offer no clues to their occupations is perhaps a reflection of the limited, non-specialised nature of such trade at this time. William son of Aldwy is possibly the son of the Adwi who witnessed the manorial survey of 1154-7, suggesting a late 12th-century date for St Leonard's at least.

As was usual with leper hospitals, St Leonard's was situated well outside the town. It adjoined the highway to Thame and Oxford on the right-hand side near the bridge over the brook (it may have been an island site) and close to the boundary with Hartwell. It gave its name to the common arable field called Spittle (i.e. hospital) field and to the Spittle mill nearby. The precise location of St John's is uncertain but an early 13th-century deed refers to two shops in the market place 'opposite the hospital of St John' and later documents seem to confirm that it adjoined the north-west corner of the market place.

Each of the two hospitals had its own endowment of property. In 1361-2 the total endowment of St Leonard's was returned as 13 acres of land and two acres of meadow in Aylesbury and Hartwell valued at 20s. The original endowment appears to have been three acres of land and two acres of meadow in Hartwell. St John's was returned at the same date as having 21 acres of land and four acres of meadow worth £1 14s., and the original endowment was 16 acres of meadow in Stoke Mandeville and Weston Turville.

More than twenty original deeds of grants made to St Leonard's survive. They date from the early 13th century to 1325 and range from as little as a single strip of land in the common fields or a rent of a penny a year to as much as two and a half acres of arable.

Some of the earliest, undated, deeds are in the form of grants to 'the leper brethren', while all the later, dated, deeds refer to 'the leper brothers and sisters', showing that women qualified for admission. In one or two later deeds a 'master and custodian' is also named. Earlier, in 1232, St Leonard's had been given royal letters of protection and letters of indulgence had also been issued in its favour. The 14th-century inquests previously mentioned claim that the right of appointing the masters of both houses belonged to the founders and their heirs, but it seems that by that time the Butlers, lords of the principal manor, were exercising the right.

Direct involvement by the monarch locally is demonstrated to some extent in the creation of several 'mini-manors', of which at least three were held directly of the king in chief by the tenure known as petty serjeantry in return for rendering more or less personal, non-military, services to the king. Over time a process of subdivision

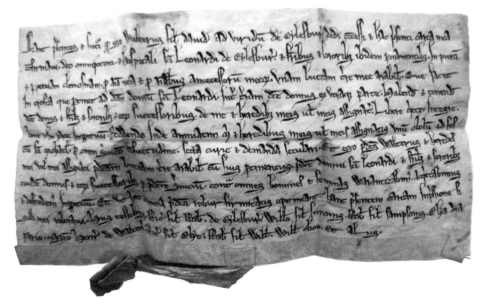

13   *Undated 13th-century grant, in Latin, to the hospital of St Leonard and to the brothers and sisters there dwelling of a butt (a small piece or ridge) of arable land. St Leonard's, founded in the 12th century, was a leper hospital.*

and subletting of the demesne plots of these and other small manors situated within the township would provide additional growth points for urban development. The best attested of the three serjeantries is the messuage, or homestead, and three virgates of land (90-120 acres of open-field arable land) known as the Otter's or, more correctly, the Otterer's Fee, granted by Henry II, a tireless devotee of the chase in all its forms, to Roger Foll, his otter hunter, around 1170. The original charter, which still survives, requires Roger in return to render to the king straw for his bed and covering for the floor of his hospice (*hospicium*), grass if he came there in summer and straw if in winter, plus two geese if in summer and three eels if in winter, to a maximum of six geese and nine eels yearly.

Otter's Fee had previously been held by Ernisius the reeve, or manorial bailiff, for the comparatively high money rent of £15 yearly. Its descent can be documented in considerable detail down to the mid-15th century, when it was absorbed into the estate of the Baldwin family. The precise location of its demesne, or home farm within the town area, is more problematic. A manorial survey of 1466 describes Otter's Fee as an apparently continuous block consisting of some 13 separate sub-tenancies, including a mill, terminating (appropriately for an otter hunter) at 'the common stream', and crossed at one point by a lane called Loterer's Lane, which on later evidence was located in the vicinity of Green End. Elsewhere it is said to lie along the king's highway. The reference to the mill and the stream show that the fee was situated at least partly on lower ground, which would seem to place it on the fringe of the west side of the town. There is also a later reference to some open-field land in Bierton belonging to the fee.

The two other early serjeantries were smaller than Otter's Fee and their history is more obscure. In a return of 1241 John Peytevin ('of Poitou') is shown as holding half a hide (up to around 50 acres) of land in Aylesbury by the service of keeping the king's pound, or pinfold, for property seized for crown debts throughout the county, rendering also 6s. at court and taking a fixed rate for each kind of livestock. Although Buckingham had pride of place in Domesday Book, Aylesbury's central position within the county made it a more convenient centre for the royal administration. The king's pinfold is one example; the county gaol is another. It stood in the market place and is mentioned as early as 1180. The county assizes were held in Aylesbury from 1218, and probably earlier, and elections of knights of the shire to Parliament were being held there by the 15th century.

At the same date William Aungevin ('of Anjou') held one virgate (around 30 acres) by the service of making summonses and distresses at the court of Aylesbury within and without the town and guarding the works (i.e. labour services) and customs due to the lord and sowing all the demesne of the manor with the lord's wheat. The surnames of the holders of these manors are a reminder that Henry II, whose empire stretched as far as the borders of Spain, had been Count of Anjou and Lord of Poitou and that post-Conquest Aylesbury had its cosmopolitan aspects.

John Peytevin's fee may perhaps be connected with the Domesday Book reference to a tenant 'who always follows the King's sheriff'. Earlier entries in the Pipe Rolls suggest that his ancestors had held it from at least as early as 1190. In 1295 it was held by William Asperville, who died the same year, and it is described as a capital messuage, 64 acres of arable, six acres of meadow and 13s. 4d. rents of free tenants. In 1329 John de Asperville conveyed this manor to Sir John de Stonore, of Stonor in Oxfordshire, whose descendants held it with other lands in Aylesbury, Walton and Stoke Mandeville until 1329, when 'Stonores Fee' together with a plot called Kings Pinfold were acquired by the Earl of Ormond, then lord of the principal manor.

Though not a serjeantry, the small manor known as the Castle Fee dates back at least to the 13th century. It seems to have been the manor held by William Graunt in 1286 and by John le Graunt in 1348, which in turn can plausibly be connected with the virgate of land held in 1198 by Roger de Sancto Mauneo, the previous tenant of which had been Robert Scot and, before him, Geoffrey de Quarrendon. By 1455 it too had come into the hands of the lord of the chief manor. In a survey of 1466, Castle Fee comprised a total of 10 messuages, including one called St John's House, two 'tenements' and a garden. Like Otter's Fee it possessed a court baron and the view of frankpledge or court leet. No other land is mentioned. The abuttals of the properties listed in the survey seem to describe an 'island' site, while elsewhere the hospital of St John Baptist is said to abut the market place. A few, much later, documents place property in the Temple Street/Temple Square area in 'Castle Fee', but no physical evidence of an actual castle has so far come to light.

Scattered references are found to other, mostly unnamed, manorial entities, including one called Ludd's Fee, incorporating the Spittle Mill, situated outside the town near the present Oxford Road, which was purchased by the Earl of Ormond from John Bascombe around 1438. The name survived into modern times as Ludd's Lane, off Whitehall Street.

Central to the settlement was the site of the former minster precinct, now transformed into the Church Fee, or manor, and forming part of the possessions of the Bishop of Lincoln, from whom it passed in 1139 to the canons of Lincoln Cathedral before being constituted a prebend in 1146 to provide the stipend of a particular canon, or prebendary (hence the name Prebendal House). Though held in free alms and exempt from secular services, in this feudal society the 'Parson's Fee', as it was later known, was looked upon as a manor like any other, with its own tenants, manor court and court leet. Significantly, however, there appears to have been very little open-field arable land attached to it. The boundaries of the manor, as recorded in the 19th century, though somewhat imprecise, show that it comprised much of the north-west half of the old town, an area of some eight to ten

14   *Nos 5-8 Parsons Fee. This row of timber-framed cottages is structurally one dwelling and is usually dated to the 17th century, but examination of the roof structure suggests a much earlier date – possibly as early as the 15th century. It was still undivided as late as the 18th century.*

acres in extent which incorporated the church and graveyard. It thus constituted much the largest single precinct as well as the most ancient.

It was on the gently sloping ground south-east of the present Kingsbury that Aylesbury's new market place, a roughly rectangular block more than twice its present size, was laid out. The reference to tolls in Domesday Book suggests that the market itself had been in existence since before 1066, though the earliest known reference to a market as such is in an extant deed of *c*.1200. Its new location was obviously carefully chosen, for it lies athwart Walton Street, which since late Saxon times had formed part of the main route to the south. Its south-eastern edge was only a few hundred yards distant from the boundary with the manor and hamlet of Walton, another Lincoln prebend from 1146. By analogy with High Wycombe, it is not unlikely that Henry II was responsible. He may also, as he appears to have done at Wycombe, have assigned blocks of land alongside the market place which could profitably be leased to larger traders, hence perhaps the persistence of quite substantial blocks of land on the perimeter of the market place, several of which later became the sites of inns.

Royal foundation would account for the absence of any mention of a market charter and also for the absence of burgage tenure, involving the creation and leasing of standard plots to traders for money rents, which came to be the norm – even the touchstone – for most markets founded by private lords in the 12th and 13th centuries by virtue of royal charters; a good example is nearby Thame, where the long curving burgage plots are still clearly traceable in the old town centre. The spaciousness of the market relative to the settlement as a whole was not in itself untypical. It left plenty of room for licensed encroachments as a means for improving the lord's rental and was in effect an alternative to the usual burgage rents.

The new market place together with the other early medieval precincts, manorial and otherwise, provided the basic framework for the development of the town in later centuries. Henceforth, until comparatively modern times, growth when it occurred was largely internal. Pressure was, of course, greatest in the market place itself, particularly on the west side, with the result that a new pattern of streets and lanes gradually emerged over the centuries. By the 14th century a similar process was at work in Kingsbury. Within the bounds of the Church Fee, too, was ample space and we know from archaeological evidence that by the 13th century the original site of the Saxon cemetery was being encroached upon.

Surviving property deeds of the 13th and early 14th centuries, many of them undated, throw some light on these developments. The fees (i.e. manors) mentioned by name, mostly prior to 1300, are the lord of Aylesbury's fee (the lord's name is usually given), Church Fee, Otter's Fee and Castle Fee. Two surviving deeds refer to shops in the market place (*forum*) of Sir John fitz Geoffrey (lord 1227-58) situated opposite the hospital of St John Baptist, and a deed of 1333 relates to two shops in the *fleshamele* (butchers' shambles). Walton Street, also in the lord's fee, figures in a deed of 1275-97. The church and the cemetery are mentioned in another. Other deeds refer to property in North Street (*in vico del North*) within the Church Fee, possibly the present Church Street, Cattesfee (Castle Street was still called Catte Street in the early 19th century) (1324), Green End in the Church Fee (1341) and Froxfield (Frogs Field) Lane (1318).

Another area of open ground, The Hale, is mentioned twice. An undated early 13th-century deed refers to a 'messuage in a corner [*angulo*] of the town called the Hale [*La Hale*], which extends to the water [i.e. the stream] south'. The Hale (Old English *healh*, a nook or corner of ground), or Hale Leys, was still an area of meadow ground much used for recreation in the early 19th century. It was destroyed by the building of the present High Street in 1826 and is commemorated by Hale Street (off Brittania Street) and by the Hale Leys shopping centre. It may have marked one of the limits of the township area. The open spaces known later as Upper and Lower Hundreds, not mentioned in the deeds, were in the same vicinity.

The earliest indication of infilling in Kingsbury is found in a deed of 1307 referring to a corner messuage there. A later deed of 1348 is a conveyance of a messuage in Kingsbury which is said to lie between two other messuages and 'extends to the highway on both sides', an apparent reference to the 'island' row which still divides Kingsbury from Buckingham Street. But, if so, how do we explain this apparent invasion of the site of the presumed principal manor house? A possible clue is provided by an undated 13th-century deed in which a certain John de Burton (i.e. of Bierton) granted to John fitz Geoffrey, lord of Aylesbury from 1227 to 1258, a messuage in the Church Fee on the north of the church. In return for this grant and for the grantor's shares in the 'fairs and markets of Aylesbury' (another copy has 'fairs and tolls') Sir John gave the enormous sum of £100. How John de Burton acquired his interest in the market is not known; clearly he was a man of some importance. This transaction would explain the otherwise puzzling fact, confirmed by later evidence, that the principal manor house, otherwise

the *Bull Inn* or *Old Bull*, was located within the boundaries of the Church Fee in the area known later as Bull Close. Evidently one outcome of the transaction was that the original Kingsbury site had become available for piecemeal development.

As previously noted, the reference to tolls in Domesday Book seems to imply that Aylesbury already had a thriving prescriptive market long before 1086 and the enlarged weekly market continued to be the focus of commerce in the town in following centuries. Aylesbury's situation at the centre of a road network and the absence of serious rival markets locally – the nearest were at Whitchurch, Wendover and Brill – ensured that it attracted custom over a wide area of surrounding countryside. King John's grant of the manor to Geoffrey fitz Peter in 1204 makes no mention of a market but, unusually, a post-1199 charter of William Marshal, 1st Earl of Pembroke (d. 1219), who was briefly regent during the minority of Henry III, tells us that he granted to Geoffrey fitz Peter his share of the market of Aylesbury, which they had divided between them. This is the earliest known reference to the market as such.

Later, in 1239, Geoffrey obtained a royal grant of a four-day annual fair commencing on the feast of St Osyth, Aylesbury's patron saint, in winter (7 October). The grant states that it was without prejudice to the existing 'ancient' customary fair held on the feast of St Osyth in summer (3 June). Such fairs were capable of attracting customers from outside the immediate district. The accounts of Merton College, Oxford for the 1290s show that regular purchases were made at Aylesbury fair including cloth for making clothes for the Master's servants and 'a white plough', the latter probably originating in the Chilterns.

Among the occupational personal names found in surviving title deeds and other records dating from the 13th and early 14th centuries, which mostly relate to small properties situate within the township, are a sprinkling which refer to trades and crafts, some of them distinctively urban. They include draper, spicer (i.e. grocer), shepherd, chamberlain, tailor, carter, salter, smith, vintner, chapman (of Walton) and goldsmith. Other names deriving from places seem to indicate a degree of inward migration. The cloth trade was evidently of some importance at this time. Records of cases brought before the itinerant justices show that 17 men in the township of Aylesbury (which was separately represented) were fined for selling cloth contrary to the assize (i.e. of inferior quality) in 1227, and in 1241 the number of similar offenders, this time listed under the heading of drapers, was 18, a much higher number than the totals for Buckingham and Wycombe.

Cases tried at assuages in 1227 give some insight into life in the town at this period. The first was one of murder. Alan, described as a merchant of Aylesbury, had been found dead 'in the field of Stoc' (Stoke Mandeville). Accused were William Cnif and two others, all of whom were found not guilty. Because Englishry had not been presented (i.e. assurance given that Alan was not a Frenchman) the murdrum fine was imposed on the township of Stoke. In another case Wiburg' of Aylesbury had appealed Ralf le Lutrier (otter hunter) and his brother William for a breach of the peace, but she had died in the interval. Because no essoin (excuse for non-appearance) had been given, her two pledges were fined. William failed to appear so he, together with five of his six pledges, who had also defaulted, were fined in their turn. William, 'earl of Mandeville' (presumably William de Mandeville, earl of Essex, lord of Aylesbury), was charged with encroaching on the king's highway. The encroachment was ordered to

be inspected and put right. A road between Ralf le Lutrier and Richard the Clerk had been blocked so that carts could not pass; this too was to be seen and corrected.

Among the cases for the hundred of Stone is a grim little tale involving persons from Aylesbury, which incidentally throws some light on aspects of everyday life locally. Edward le foc of Aylesbury and his wife Matilda were accused, along with William de Burnham, of the murder of Matilda, daughter of William le Paumer, and her son and of a poor woman lodging with them. The crime had been committed at Ford in the parish of Dinton. The jurors found that the accused Matilda had conspired with her brother Thomas, a chaplain of London, to commit the murder with the help of William de Burnham, apparently in order to prevent the deceased woman from marrying their brother, John de Biry. The jurors testified that on the night in question Matilda and William de Burnham went forth from Aylesbury in the direction of the hamlet of Ford:

William bore a staff and the watchmen of the town of Aylesbury asked them where they were going and they replied, to Ford where they wished to speak with a friend and on the following morning when they returned the watch on seeing them asked whence they had come. They replied 'from their friend'. But William no longer had his staff. The jury say that when Matilda who was slain sought John for her husband, John presented her with many goods and bought for her a cloak and a tunic at the fair of Aylesbury [evidently the 'old fair' on the third of June]. Whereupon Thomas the chaplain and Matilda his sister came and used threatening words to the effect that it was no use his buying a tunic for her because before she could use it she would be burnt or have died some other death, and it was no use buying a cloak because, in short, she would have no neck from which to hang it ...

15 (Left) The present parish church of St Mary's dates from the 13th and 14th centuries though there is evidence that there had been an Anglo-Saxon church on the same site. Heavily restored by Sir George Gilbert Scott in the 19th century, it retains much of its imposing medieval proportions.

16 (Right) The south aisle of St Mary's showing the medieval central oak pier and ceiling. It was in this area of the church that the ecclesiastical courts for the archdeaconry are thought to have been held. Their jurisdiction included matrimonial causes and the probate of wills.

The judgement was that Matilda should be burnt, William hanged and Thomas, the chaplain, outlawed.

One of the most important developments of the 13th and early 14th centuries was the building – or rather rebuilding, for it was clearly not the first – of the parish church. Although heavily restored in the 19th century, it was from the first an exceptionally large and imposing cruciform church with central tower. Unusually, it was all of one build in the Early English style apart from a few, mainly early 14th-century, chapels, etc. Changes after this were mostly to windows and other relatively small details. Cruciform churches are not numerous in Buckinghamshire and are mostly associated with towns or places that had markets, and it must have taken up to half a century to complete. Older than the church itself is the beautiful circular stone baptismal font, which dates from the late 12th century and is presumably a relic of a previous parish church. Its design was

17   *The upper section of the original 'perpendicular' east window of St Mary's, which was replaced during the Victorian restoration and now stands in the grounds of the nearby Green End House.*

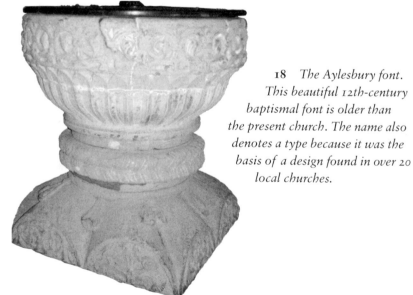

18   *The Aylesbury font. This beautiful 12th-century baptismal font is older than the present church. The name also denotes a type because it was the basis of a design found in over 20 local churches.*

19 *Late 13th-century stone carving of the Madonna and Child. This rare survival stood for many years, invisible from the ground, in a small niche high up in the west front of St Mary's. Brought down in the 1970s, its exceptional quality went unrecognised until the mid-1980s.*

20 *Medieval piscina (holy water stoup) showing carved relief head.*

21a and b *These carved stone grotesques, now concealed from view in the recesses of the parish church, are witness to a rich vein of medieval masonic fantasy.*

22 *This detached example is evidently post-medieval but is in the same tradition.*

the basis of some 22 so-called 'Aylesbury' fonts in the locality.

The church is well above the average in size, the nave alone comprising around 2,000 square feet. This suggests a large congregation and may reflect the fact that until the 1290s Aylesbury had several appurtenant chapelries. Its size also made the church the natural venue for synods and visitations held for the archdeaconry of Buckingham and it was also the place where ecclesiastical courts for the archdeaconry were held for many centuries. The stone used is rather poor quality soft limestone, probably brought from Totternhoe, near Luton in Bedfordshire, a distance of some twenty miles. The cost of transportation alone would have been enormous. The assumption must be that the expense of building the church fell mainly upon the parishioners, though the lord of the principal manor may well have contributed and the link with Lincoln Cathedral is likely to have been significant, at any rate in relation to design and expertise.

Since the prebendary was, almost by definition, an absentee, the service of the church had to be carried on by others; only in 1274 was a formal vicarage ordained. Under this arrangement the vicar received a modest endowment of land, or glebe, and the right to receive the less valuable 'small' tithes of the parish. The vicars were supposed to be resident. Later, in 1294, Bierton, Buckland and Stoke Mandeville, hitherto chapelries of Aylesbury, were constituted separate parishes.

The proximity of the church to the gaol was to create problems for the authorities, for any felon who could find refuge within a church and claim sanctuary was entitled to 'abjure the realm' and thereby obtain a safe conduct overseas. Since security at the gaol was low and the gaolers often suspect, it is hardly surprising that evidence from the late 14th century shows that it was not unusual for escaped prisoners to elude death by this route.

Three

LATE MEDIEVAL AYLESBURY:
THE BUTLERS, AN ANGLO-IRISH LORDSHIP

On the death without issue of Richard Lord Fitz John in 1297 the partly illegible 'extent', or brief survey, attached to the formal inquisition post mortem states that he held the manor of Aylesbury with the hamlet of Burton (Bierton) of the king in chief by the service of one knight's fee and that it comprised a capital messuage (dwelling) and a room or hall (*camera*) next to the church of Aylesbury; 454 acres of arable land and 237 acres of meadow on the wold (*super waldam*) which can be mown in a wet summer but not in a dry; a fishery; a windmill; a second mill; various rents; and a fair on the feast of St Osyth; all valued at £51 4s. 6d.

Aylesbury was assigned in dower for life to Richard's widow Emma, who married Robert de Montalt (d. 1329), hereditary steward of Chester and a leading feudal magnate. The inheritance of the estate was divided among Richard's four sisters. Thus, on Emma's death in around 1332 Aylesbury, with other lands, descended to James Butler, Earl of Ormond, as the grandson and heir of Joan Butler, the youngest of the sisters. James died in 1338, having first settled Aylesbury on his wife Eleanor de Bohun for life.

Eleanor de Bohun was the daughter of Humphrey de Bohun (d. 1322), 7th Earl of Hereford. As the granddaughter of Edward I and a cousin of Edward III she was also in the highest rank of the English aristocracy. Her marriage in 1328 to the youthful James Butler (c.1305-38), a powerful Anglo-Irish lord who was created 1st Earl of Ormond the same year and whose principal seat was Kilkenny Castle, was thus an event of great dynastic significance. The Butlers, who held Aylesbury for most of the remainder of the Middle Ages, were to be absentee landlords throughout.

By 1338, still in his early thirties, the earl was dead, but not before he had settled Aylesbury on his young wife, the mother of his infant son and heir, another James, born in 1331. It would remain in her exclusive possession until her death in 1363, a period of some 25 years which witnessed immense social and economic change throughout England, brought about in large part by the effects of the Black Death of 1348 and following years. In Aylesbury it was also a period when a greater volume of surviving documentation became available, including some manorial accounts which, although far from abundant and concerned only indirectly with the manorial tenants, nevertheless enable us to form a fuller picture of community life in general and of manorial administration in particular. How much of her time Eleanor spent in Aylesbury is unknown. At least one

23 *These carved effigies in the church of St Mary's at Gowran, near Kilkenny, are thought to represent James Butler, 1st Earl of Ormond (c.1305-1338), a powerful Anglo-Irish lord, and his wife Eleanor de Bohun (d. 1363). Under her husband's will the countess acquired the manor of Aylesbury for her lifetime.*

document issued in her name is dated 'from my castle at Kilpeck', in Herefordshire, where the remains of a rather modest motte and bailey castle are still visible close to the renowned Norman parish church. Kilpeck may well have been her principal residence but it was still normal in this period for aristocratic lords and their retinues to be frequently on the move among their various residences.

Eleanor's relation with her Aylesbury tenants began badly. In July 1342 a judicial commission was issued to enquire into

her complaint that certain named men of Aylesbury, about 35 in number, had depastured cattle on her crops and grass and had assaulted her men and servants. Later in the same year a second commission alleged that a certain Augustine Bever and 12 others (not all of whom were named in the first commission), having formed a sworn conspiracy to maintain their illegal doings, had assaulted Eleanor's steward, John de Colyngton, and when the latter had taken refuge in the church had broken the doors and windows in upon him and imprisoned him and forced him to release them from trespasses which they had committed and to swear that he would quit the service of the Countess. The accused were stated to be now 'common malefactors vagabond in the said county'.

The outcome of this dispute is not known. Several of the individuals mentioned and most of the surnames occur as parties to property deeds of the period and, since the names of two of them (Ralph le Draper and Richard atte Merssh) recur after 1342, it appears that at least some of those involved succeeded in making their peace. In 1344, too, a royal pardon was granted to a certain William de Caldecote, who had been outlawed in connection with trespasses and confederacies committed in Aylesbury. The dispute reflects a growing pressure on land in a period of rapidly increasing population. The grassland in question was possibly the pasture called Haydon Hill (now a housing estate), which was to be the subject of disputes between lord and tenants in later centuries, rather than the water meadows on the flood plain. A 16th-century document notes that the physical evidence of ridge and furrow at Haydon Hill proved that it had not always been under grass and the accounts seem to confirm this. As in all such disputes, we may be sure that, from the tenants' point of view, it was the Countess who was at fault in seeking to deprive them of what they considered to be their customary rights.

Nor were all the tenants simple peasants. Some had occupational names such as draper (three), tailor and roper, but almost everyone in Aylesbury, whatever their principal employment, would have had some stake, however small, in the land. The reference to drapers confirms that the cloth trade was still to the fore. Chapman and taverner are among the surnames of the townsmen who attested a tax on church property in 1342, and the tax of a 15th on moveable goods levied the same year produced a total of £1 9s. 8d. from 'merchants, cattle dealers and other traders of Aylesbury for the products of their lands and store of wool, &c.'.

Trade in English wool at this period had already assumed international proportions (wool from the Cotswolds was especially esteemed). The outbreak of war with France in 1338, the start of what was later to be styled the Hundred Years' War, led Edward III (1327-77) to seize stocks of wool from merchants and to organise the collection of grain for the provisioning of his armies, and Aylesbury figures in both connections. We find, for example, a reference in the official government records to a debt of £572 – an enormous sum – owed by the king to Robert le Spicer (d. 1339?) of Aylesbury, who, with other merchants, had been given a monopoly of the sale of wool in 1337, and Aylesbury was also one of the places where granaries were being established for the king's military service.

A survey of the manorial demesne, or home farm, taken in 1342-3, a few years before the great plague, shows that it comprised 490 acres of arable and 414 acres of meadow, a high proportion of the total agricultural land of the manor. It represents a total increase of 213 acres (36 of it pasture) over 1297. The arable is located in named furlongs but the names of the great open fields in which the furlongs would have been located are not given. In the survey the manor house is described as a 'barton' (i.e. a demesne farmstead) called Justicebury, 'which is the place of the capital messuage', occupying four and a half acres. The buildings are said to be worth 13s. 4d. a year and a vacant plot next to the churchyard which used to render 6s. 8d. is now worth only 18d. because not built upon. The name Justicebury is an unusual one and suggests a place in which justice is administered. Later evidence suggests that it stood on the north-west edge of Kingsbury, the presumed site of Henry II's *hospitium* which had evidently become a public space in late medieval times. Also listed are a windmill and a horse mill, each worth 60s. a year, a fishery from a weir (no value assigned) and the proceeds of the courts, market and annual nine-day fair (5-13 October).

Manorial accounts for 1350-1 also mention a dovehouse and a rabbit warren, as well as listing expenses for horses stabled and

24 *Jug or pitcher, part of a collection of 13th- to 14th-century pottery found in a pit in Buckingham Street in 1963. The nearby villages of Brill and Boarstall in were major suppliers of pottery throughout the Middle Ages.*

fed, including the Countess's three palfreys and her pack horses and horses belonging to a number of named individuals. One of the individuals concerned was [Sir] John Chastillon of Thornton, currently sheriff of Buckinghamshire and Bedfordshire (the offices were combined), and there is also a back payment on behalf of William Croiser, dating from the time he was sheriff in 1346-7. These two payments suggest that the manor house may have been supplying accommodation for the sheriffs on a regular basis while on official business, hence perhaps the name Justicebury.

The Black Death was at its height in Buckinghamshire between May and September of 1349. Information about its impact is patchy, but it is known that at least 87 members of the parochial clergy died. At Salden in the parish of Mursley all but one of the manorial tenants were reported dead and at Winslow analysis of a run of court rolls indicates a 30 per cent mortality. Yet, strangely, the earliest of several surviving Aylesbury manorial account rolls, which covers the period September 1350 to May 1351, makes no direct comment on the pestilence, though a laconic entry cites 'excessive rain' and 'lack of people' (*defectus populi*) as reasons for the low yield of crops recorded. The longer term effects of the plague on the economy of the town are perhaps best illustrated by the apparent decline in the lord's revenues from the tolls of the market and fairs. The 1342-3 survey values the tolls of the market at £23, those of the fairs at £5 and the profits of the manor courts at over £16. This compares with the figure of £10 for tolls given in an account roll for 1377, which seems to include the takings of the fairs and courts as well.

On the death of Countess Eleanor in 1363 Aylesbury reverted to her son James Butler (1331-82), 2nd Earl of Ormond, called the Noble Earl because he was of the blood royal

through his mother. Born and brought up in Ireland, James was the only Irish magnate with extensive estates in England, and thus a figure of great importance in Anglo-Irish relations, especially as the family had a record of consistent loyalty to the English Crown. Aylesbury was now once again a unit in a large estate of up to 70 manors scattered throughout England including two other Buckinghamshire manors, Great Linford and Twyford.

The administration of the demesne lands and perquisites was the responsibility of the manorial bailiff, who in a large manor such as Aylesbury was usually an important personage in his own right. From as early as 1340 the Countess Eleanor was in the habit of leasing the tolls of markets and fairs and the profits of courts to her current bailiff for several years at a time. Then in 1357 she granted a seven-year lease of the manor house with all its demesne lands, etc., to Ralph Northgate, bailiff. The lease was renewed by the 2nd Earl in 1364 and again in 1366. However, it appears that direct exploitation of the demesne was not finally abandoned until after 1382.

The 2nd Earl evidently had a special interest in Aylesbury, for shortly before his death, from his castle of Knocktopher in Kilkenny in 1382, he granted 10 acres of land in the town as a site for a Franciscan friary. The gift was eventually ratified in 1391 by his son, the 3rd Earl, another James, who augmented the original 10 acres by the purchase of existing smallholdings to form a compact block of some 15 acres or more stretching from the present Rickfords Hill to the California Brook and from Walton Street almost to the Oxford Road. Some of this land was later leased out by the friars in small lots to tenants.

By 1396 a permanent church was in course of erection, when Alice Giffard, widow of Sir John Giffard of Twyford (she

25   *Aylesbury's Franciscan friary originated in a gift of land by the 2nd Earl of Ormond in 1382, but its church and other buildings were still incomplete at the end of the century. These two 15th-century statuettes carved in Nottingham alabaster were dug up at Rickford's Hill near the traditional site.*

had had two other husbands, one of whom had been a merchant), gave the large sum of a hundred marks (£66 13s. 4d.) towards the works. The following year another benefactor, a merchant of Winchester called Stephen Haym, gave 10 times that amount towards the cost of the church, cloister and other conventual buildings. These appear to have been located not far from the market place in the vicinity of the house formerly called the Friarage at the corner of Rickfords Hill and the lane now called Friars Passage. It seems possible that Richard II may have been instrumental in obtaining Haym's munificent donation, for the Aylesbury friars distinguished themselves by remaining loyal to Richard after his deposition and one of them suffered execution for boldly telling Henry IV to his face that he was not the rightful king, but merely the Duke of Lancaster.

The house was a small one, but as members of a mendicant order of preachers the friars in their distinctive grey robes must have become a familiar part of the everyday scene in Aylesbury and its environs. Essentially an urban order, they were supposed to support themselves by alms and not to own property, but by the late 14th century this rule had evidently been relaxed somewhat. The popularity of the Aylesbury friars is shown by numerous bequests to them in local wills as late as the 1530s. No trace of their convent now remains.

26   *Recumbent statue of an unidentified late 14th-century knight in St Mary's in the parish church. It is thought to have been removed from the church of the friary.*

Hitherto the Butlers seem to have confined their political activities to Ireland, where the 3rd Earl (c.1360-1405) was viceroy and exercised an almost sovereign jurisdiction within his own territories. This had begun to change by 1447 when, a few years before his death in 1452, the 4th Earl of Ormond gave Aylesbury to his eldest son and heir, Sir James Butler, then aged 27. Young James was connected to the powerful Beaufort family through his wife Eleanor, daughter of the Duke of Somerset. In 1449 he was created Earl of Wiltshire in the English peerage, in recognition of his zealous support for the Lancastrian cause, and in March 1455 he was appointed Lord High Treasurer of England.

Wiltshire's acquisition of Aylesbury was accompanied by changes in the administration of the estate. Henceforth, instead of being leased to a single tenant as had become customary, it was entrusted to a salaried agent, or 'approver', and his accounts show that the demesne arable and meadow were let piecemeal annually, as appears to have happened earlier also.

In addition, manorial buildings, including the moot hall, or market house, the warren and the dovehouse, were repaired and refurbished at considerable expense. The manor house, presumably the former Justicebury (the name is last noted in 1357), had been converted into an inn called the *Bull*, or the *Old Bull*, and enlarged. It looks as if the Earl intended Aylesbury to be one of his power bases (his principal base was in Wiltshire). Manorial accounts for this period include a bill for the cost of maintaining 65 of his own and his servants' horses for 24 days, together with a squire and five grooms to look after them.

An incomplete rental of the manor dating from the 1450s contains references to lanes or 'rows' called butchers, cordwainers (i.e. shoemakers and leather workers), bakers and drapers, according to trade, all evidently created by licensed encroachments on the south-west side of the market place. Kingsbury is mentioned and there are also references to Green End and to the rother (i.e. oxen and cattle) fair, the latter seemingly denoting an area at

27 *Market towns such as Aylesbury abounded in inns and taverns. The* King's Head, *off Market Square, is the town's oldest surviving inn and is renowned for its 15th-century stained-glass windows incorporating the arms of Henry VI and his queen.*

the lower end of the market place, where horse fairs were still being held in the early 20th century. No fewer than six inns or taverns are mentioned, though not all paid rent to the manor. They were the *King's Head*, the *George*, the *Bell* – all located in the market place – and the *Bull* and the *Swan* in Kingsbury. The *Bell* was in existence by the late 14th century, probably on its present site, as it abutted the friarage land. The *King's Head* was relatively new and was not actually an inn at this period, having been built as a private residence by the father of William Wandesford, or Waynsford, another Lancastrian notable who served in the household of Henry IV's consort, Queen Margaret of Anjou, but it incorporated a tavern at basement level, as found in some contemporary London establishments, and paid rent for its sign. Now owned by the National Trust, the *King's Head* is Aylesbury's only surviving medieval building of its kind, though a number of smaller dwellings survive.

The weekly market attracted buyers and sellers from Aylesbury's agricultural hinterland in the Vale, as well as from Wycombe (famed for its corn market),

28   *The cobbled King's Head Lane is an example of the effects of the gradual infilling of the adjacent market place.*

29   *Artist's impression of the whole inn complex.*

Amersham, Chesham and other places in the Chilterns. It thus continued to provide a place of exchange between the two contrasting economies. The town's importance as a source of provisions is evidenced by the numbers of retailers fined for minor transgressions in the manor court. In a rare surviving roll for 1454-5 up to 10 butchers, six bakers, 15 fishmongers, 29 ale sellers, 16 brewers and four innkeepers were fined in a single session. These figures are roughly on a par with what they were a century later. One or two of the fishmongers and, more surprisingly, of the bakers, were outsiders. More surprisingly still, archaeological evidence shows that no fewer than 12 species of sea fish were consumed in the town in medieval times. Apart from agriculture, service trades predominated in Aylesbury's economy. Of craft trades the most important were evidently the shoemakers and leather workers. There were no craft guilds, but the shoemakers as a body paid to have a favourable site to display their wares on market days.

Of course, Aylesbury merchants also took their wares to other neighbouring markets. A later court roll tells the sad story of how John Walker, an Aylesbury glover, met his death by falling into a hole which a certain Richard Boose, a baker, had dug in the street called Bierton Way during John's absence at Leighton Buzzard market, in order to extract clay with which to repair his windmill. John's horse loaded with his glover's panniers first fell in and John was drowned trying to rescue it.

In 1450 Aylesbury acquired an important new parish institution when the Guild or Fraternity of the Blessed Virgin Mary was incorporated by royal licence, though there is some reason to think that it had been in existence for some considerable time before that date. It was formally sponsored by Cardinal Kemp, then Lord Chancellor of England. The seven other founders include three members of the rising Baldwin family, eminent lawyers, who had long associations with the Butlers and with the wider administration of their English estates as members of their council. Their possessions included the *Crown* inn in the market place, which appears to have been their principal residence, and the small manors of Castle Fee and Otter's Fee in Aylesbury

30   *Founded in 1450, the guild or fraternity of the Blessed Virgin Mary soon became one of Aylesbury most cherished institutions. Its dissolution in 1547 was a great loss to the town. Its Brotherhood House has been partly preserved within the fabric of Ceely House in Church Street, now part of the County Museum. Shown are fragments of the original wall decorations.*

31 *Rose noble coin of Edward IV, one of four found in an upright beam of the Brotherhood House during conversion work at Ceely House in 1952. It belongs to a type issued in 1469-70. Left, obverse; right, reverse.*

and Bawd's Fee in Walton. The royal licence empowered the fraternity to hold corporate property to the value of £20, an important privilege.

Such lay fraternities were very popular in late medieval times. They were found in all towns of any size and some also had members over a wide stretch of countryside who shared in its spiritual benefits. The Aylesbury fraternity's objects were purely religious and charitable, the principal one being to employ a priest to maintain the daily celebration of mass for the souls of members past and present, but (as often happened) over the years as it accumulated property and prestige it became a focus for the economic and social life of the town and to some extent of its immediate neighbourhood. As late as May 1534, for example, Sir Edward Don of Horsenden, a local notable, records that he spent 20d. at Aylesbury 'to the fraternyte dyner'. By 1500 the three annually elected wardens had become responsible for holding one of the three keys to the chest containing the court rolls of the manor, the other key-holders being the homage of the manor court, known collectively as 'the 22 and the 12', and the manorial bailiff. By 1486, too, the fraternity had acquired responsibility for the two hospitals. Around 1472 a new Brotherhood House in which to hold meetings was erected near the church. Much of this two-storey, timber-framed building has survived within the fabric of Ceely House, now part of the

County Museum in Church Street, and some of its interior decorative scheme has been uncovered.

Meanwhile both the Earl of Wiltshire and his fellow Lancastrian William Wandesford had been caught up in the Wars of the Roses. Wiltshire was captured at the Battle of Towton and summarily beheaded a few weeks later. He and his two brothers were attainted of high treason and their estates were forfeited to the crown. Aylesbury was later re-granted to Henry Bourchier, the recently created Earl of Essex and uncle to the new king, Edward IV, and his wife Isabel and it remained in his hands for the rest of the Yorkist period. Wandesford's property, including the *King's Head*, was acquired by Sir Ralph Verney, a local Yorkist with London connections, who also owned property in Fleet Marston and Middle Claydon.

It was during this period that John Balky was bailiff. His surviving notebook, though not always easy to interpret, is a valuable source of information about the workings of the manor in his time, including details of repairs done to the *Bull* inn, the moot (i.e. assembly) hall, the Spittle Mill and the windmill. Like his predecessors in office, Balky was a man of considerable substance and was one of the earliest wardens of the fraternity. His house was on the site of the present *Harrow* public house and this part of the town was at one time known as Balky's Town End, indicating the limit of the urban area (there was also a Lomes Town End, of uncertain location), and it seems likely that Bakers' Lane, the old name for Cambridge Street, was actually a corruption of his name. His duties required him *inter alia* to ride as far as Coventry for the annual autumn audit and also to London three times a year to deliver the customary fee farm rent due from the manor.

The 1490s were notable for acts of practical charity by private individuals which brought long-term benefits to the town. Sir Hugh Clopton (d. 1496), of Stratford-on-Avon, who had made his career in London (he was Lord Mayor of London in 1492), is commemorated in the gild hall of Stratford as having made a causeway '3 miles from Aylesbury towards London and 1 mile on this side'. The wording suggests that Sir Hugh had the interests of his fellow townsmen particularly in mind. Among his beneficiaries (assuming that he favoured this route over the Oxford–High Wycombe one) would have been William Shakespeare, who was to purchase Clopton's former Stratford residence, then known as New Place, in 1597. Clopton's causeway evidently incorporated Walton Street, the bad state of which had been a constant source of problems in earlier centuries. Another benefactor was a local man, John Stone, proprietor of the *George* inn, who in 1494 left some property in Green End for the erection and maintenance of a public clock on Aylesbury parish church. It was, so far as is known, the earliest public clock in Buckinghamshire and can be seen as symbolising a new, more modern, attitude to time.

Even more munificent than either of these was John Bedford, an Aylesbury lawyer holding an office in the central courts in London, who died in 1494, leaving the income from his considerable property in the town, partly for the upkeep of the highways within the lordship of Aylesbury and partly to give relief 'to blind people, to crook, sick, feeble and poor people' of the town. Unfortunately the gift, which was conditional on the failure of his own direct heirs (his wife survived until the 1540s), was fraudulently converted to other uses and did not take effect until nearly a century after his death. Both as a beneficial institution and as a source of political patronage, Bedford's charity was to play a significant role in the town's history.

After the defeat of the Yorkist cause at the Battle of Bosworth in 1485 and the accession of Henry Tudor, inheritor of the Lancastrian claims, as Henry VII, Aylesbury was restored to Wiltshire's younger brother, Thomas, 7th Earl of Ormond, who died in 1515 leaving a very large bequest of £65 6s. to the friary. He was the last of the Butlers in the legitimate male line and Aylesbury accordingly descended to his daughter Margaret, wife of Sir William Boleyn, a wealthy Kentish landowner; their daughter Anne was Henry VIII's future queen. The will made in 1518 by the Earl of Wiltshire's former bailiff, Christopher Dawson (d. 1520), a man of wealth and status (he was lessee of the Spittle Mill), is redolent of medieval Catholic piety. It includes the sum of £30 for an honest priest to sing before the image of the Blessed Lady in the Lady chapel in Aylesbury church and to assist in the services of the chancel there for the space of five years, 10 shillings to the fraternity and 10 marks (£3 6s. 8d.) for a priest to sing 'where my lord of Ormonde lieth buried'.

Four

TUDOR AND EARLY STUART

On the evidence of the muster roll compiled in 1522, combined with that of the subsidy (tax) roll of 1524-5, Aylesbury in the early 16th century was a relatively prosperous place, at any rate in the hierarchy of Buckinghamshire towns, ranking just second to Wycombe in terms of total wealth and with an estimated total population of 800 to 1,000 (exclusive of Walton). This figure sounds tiny to modern ears but was larger than many – perhaps the majority – of contemporary market towns. A total of 26.7 per cent of taxpayers were assessed on goods or wages worth £1 per annum; 40 per cent at between £1 and £2 (a group that included small peasant farmers and less-skilled craftsmen); while of the remaining 34 per cent only five per cent were taxed at £20 or above. On the other hand, the top five per cent accounted for 43.4 per cent of the total tax paid, evidence that the relative prosperity was very unevenly distributed. The three masters of the fraternity were all substantial citizens, assessed at £10, £16 and £20 respectively.

The will, made in 1534, of Robert Breckett, one of the better-off townsmen who was assessed at £20 (reduced from £40) on his goods, shows that, like many others, he had several irons in the fire. In addition to owning a drapery shop, he had property in Aylesbury and Bierton

and a lease of the *White Hart* inn in the market place. One of his younger sons was attending the grammar school (he does not say where). But by far the wealthiest man in Aylesbury, and one of the five wealthiest in Buckinghamshire in terms of his goods, was John Collingbourne, described elsewhere as 'yeoman alias woolpacker alias woolman', who was assessed at £201. He bequeathed 32 acres of land to the fraternity.

The gulf between rich and poor appears to have been widening and there is evidence that poverty was becoming a serious social problem locally. In a deed of 1534 Sir John Baldwin refers to the 'many poor folk of the said town' who were unable to contribute to the repair of the church and in 1545 his daughter, Alice Baldwin (she was the last abbess of Burnham), left the large sum of £20 to the poor 'specially in Aylesbury where I think great need is'. Other testators left money to the poor's box and to the poor in general.

There is little to suggest that the state of religion in the parish in the 1520s and 1530s gave cause for serious concern. It was common, for example, for parishioners to leave sums of money in their wills (often witnessed by the parish clergy) for the upkeep of lights before the images of particular saints in the parish church. The 1522 muster roll lists five resident priests,

32 No 23 Castle Street, shown in this old photograph in use as a coal merchant's office and coal yard, was originally a timber-framed Tudor farmhouse with house and outbuildings under one roof. It has since been restored as a dwelling.

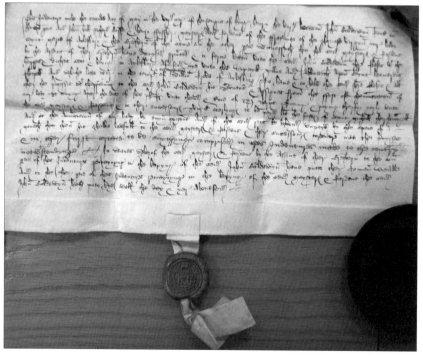

33 Lease, in English, from the master and wardens of the Fraternity of Our Lady, and the brethren, to John Baldwin, gentleman, of land 'nigh unto the Spittle milne and abutting upon St Leonard's chapel' for 21 years at an annual rent of 18s., 1516. The wax seal is intact.

34 *Parsons Fee, lower end, showing (right) the gable of St Osyth's (c.1700), the former prebendal farm, and its two 16th- and 17th-century timber-framed former barns, converted into dwellings. The 16th-century prebendal tithe barn, now used as a warehouse, is round the corner in Castle Street.*

35 *Wooden 'nail' removed from the concealed timber framing of a Tudor house on the corner of Bourbon Street and Temple Street, demolished 1974. The demolition revealed a section of the Iron Age hillfort ditch.*

one of whom is described as a curate. The vicar, Dr Nicholas Miles (Mylys), was an absentee. His successor, Dr John Lush, was, however, clearly resident in 1534. At a visitation held in 1533 (the year of Henry VIII's marriage to Anne Boleyn) the churchwardens and leading parishioners requested the vicar to warn the people to behave more reverently in service time and specifically to kneel at the elevation (of the host), but otherwise found little amiss.

Sir John Baldwin purchased the manor from Anne Boleyn's father in 1538. Two years earlier Baldwin had been the presiding judge at the Queen's trial. He was the town's very first resident lord and in 1541 he obtained a grant of the property of the recently suppressed friary and converted the conventual buildings into an appropriate residence. He also rebuilt the market house, which did duty

36 *An 18th-century print of the Tudor town hall, or market house, erected by Sir John Baldwin, lord of the manor (d. 1547). It had several successors.*

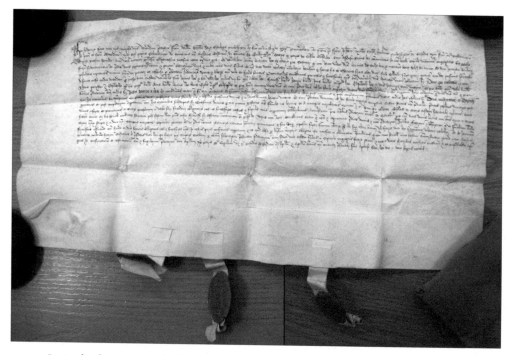

37 *Latin deed, 1533, by which the Aylesbury friars undertake regularly to offer up various specified intercessory prayers for Dame Lettice Lee, her husband Sir Robert Lee (knight of Quarrendon, d. 1539), and others, in return for benefits received and for repairs to their house. Neither party could have known that in less than five years the friary would have ceased to exist.*

as a sessions house as well. Early in 1537, while the dissolution of the monasteries was already in progress, Baldwin had reported to Thomas Cromwell that there had been rumours that Buckingham and Padbury churches were to be pulled down and of a plan afoot to resist, and that a baker's boy of Aylesbury had claimed that the jewels of Aylesbury church were to be 'fetched away'. The rumours were wide of the mark, for Henry's ire was reserved for monastic foundations, but they are suggestive of popular loyalty to the existing religious order and of fears for the future.

The suppression of the Aylesbury friary, which took place in early 1538, was carried out with great brutality; the friars (there were only nine of them at this date) were

not simply dismissed but were compelled to abase themselves by publicly denouncing their former way of life. The effect of this on most of the inhabitants has to be imagined. Worse was to come with the sudden introduction of a thoroughgoing Protestant reformation during the reign of the boy-king Edward VI (1547-53). Even more traumatic than the loss of the friary must have been the dissolution of the fraternity in 1547, which deprived the town of one of its most cherished institutions and of all the property, including the almshouses and hospitals, which it held in trust for the benefit of the townsfolk. A few years later, in 1552, came the enforced 'stripping of the altars' of the parish churches and the confiscation of their treasures. This reign also saw serious disturbances related to

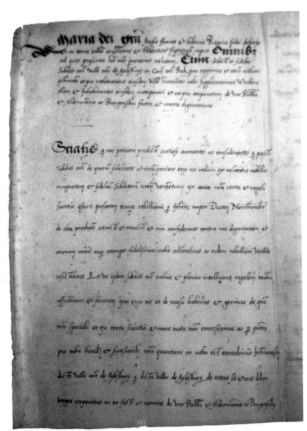

38 *Royal charter of incorporation, 1554. This contemporary paper version of Queen Mary's charter was evidently the working copy of the clerk to the new corporation, Anthony Hornyold (he was also county coroner). The original engrossed charter was allegedly misappropriated by the Pakingtons, lords of the manor, and the corporation proved short-lived.*

39 *The original binding of the copy charter. It consists of an illuminated parchment bifolium from a medieval service book containing part of the Latin liturgy for the Holy Week ceremonies.*

enclosures in nearby parishes including Quainton, Oving and Pitchcott.

The third and fourth quarters of the 16th century were marked – in Aylesbury as in many other places – by rampant inflation, outbreaks of epidemic disease and of communal strife, related at least in part to the enclosure of common lands. But the antiquary John Leland (d. 1552) describes the town as 'a celebrate market' and William Camden, another antiquary, who visited the town in 1586, found it 'a very fair Market-town, large and pretty populous, surrounded with a great number of pleasant meadows and pastures'. He noted that 'The greatest repute it now hath is for cattel' and remarked on the vast numbers of sheep grazed at Quarrendon and elsewhere in the district, the sequel in many cases to large-scale enclosure of arable over the preceding century and more, often – as at Quarrendon, where the Lee family were the landlords – accompanied by depopulation. Social and economic forces were gradually bringing about a more commercial form of agriculture in Aylesbury and its hinterland and as a result many smallholders were being squeezed out and the problem of poverty was increasing.

Aylesbury benefited from the general expansion of inland trading in the second half of the century. A return of inns and ale-houses in Buckinghamshire in 1577 credits the town with four innkeepers, two vint-ners and 25 alehouses, the largest combined total for any town in the county, though Stony Stratford, situated on the Great North Road, had more inns. The continu-ing growth of county administration was also to the town's commercial advantage, for Aylesbury, with its central position in the county, maintained its edge over the rival claims of Buckingham as the meeting place for quarter sessions and assize courts and the seat of the county gaol.

Any hopes that Sir John Baldwin had of founding a dynasty were dashed by the death of his only son without a male heir, and on his own death in 1545 his estate descended to his two grandchildren, one of whom, Sir Thomas Pakington, knight, of Hampton Lovett in Worcestershire, even-tually obtained sole possession of Aylesbury in 1551. Pakington's accession was the signal for the outbreak of a bitter dispute between lord and tenants over grazing rights in the lord's pasture at Haydon Hill. The tenants, who seem to have comprised the majority of the townspeople, produced a written customal (almost certainly fabricated) as evidence of their traditional rights to have access to Haydon Hill at certain seasons and at fixed preferential rates, the real value of which had been greatly reduced by inflation. Chancery litigation followed,

40   Page from the earliest Aylesbury parish register, 1565-1667, showing entries for the years 1583-4.

but in the meantime the Pakingtons appear to have remained in possession.

At this point events in national politics came to the aid of the townsmen when in January 1554 Aylesbury was granted a charter of incorporation by the Catholic Queen Mary (one of 44 such charters granted during Mary's short reign). It was ostensibly a reward for the town's loyalty in rallying to Mary's support during the rebellion of the Duke of Northumberland, whose daughter-in-law Lady Jane Grey had been proclaimed queen in various places on the death of Edward VI in July 1553. This period had in fact seen widespread unrest in Buckinghamshire and neighbouring counties. Completely ignoring the existing rights of the lord of the manor, the new charter established a corporate borough, naming as bailiff John Walwyn, 'gentleman', a relative newcomer to the town and a prime mover in the dispute over Haydon Hill, as well as nine other aldermen and 12 principal burgesses, a self-perpetuating body of twenty-two. Two of the 10 aldermen are styled esquire and three gentleman, of whom three were lawyers by profession; the occupations of the other five are unknown, but all appear to have been possessed of some landed property locally. The avocations of the capital burgesses were more plebeian, including two husbandmen, two butchers, a 'fisher', a tallow chandler (grocer) and a shoemaker.

The new corporation did not last long. Much later it was alleged that the Pakingtons prevented it from exercising its rights by means of protracted Chancery lawsuits and it is possible that a Privy Council letter dated as late as 1593 referring to 'some controversy' between Pakington and his Aylesbury tenants may refer to the charter as well as to Haydon Hill, which is not specified in the charter. We know, too, that an epidemic in the late 1550s carried off a disproportionate number of the original councillors. There is evidence that Walwyn had at least two successors, but after that nothing more is heard of the institution as such.

But though the corporation itself did not survive, the charter left one very important legacy, for the town's right to be represented by two Members of Parliament, which it conferred, was too valuable a privilege to let go. Ironically, the immediate beneficiaries were the Pakingtons, who were able to arrogate to themselves the effective nomination of the two representatives without the tiresome (and potentially expensive) necessity of actually holding an election. The return made by Lady Dorothy Pakington, then lady of the manor, to the writ of election for the parliament called in 1572 makes it explicit that she herself had chosen the two representatives for *her* town of Aylesbury. Over time this control of elections was gradually eroded, but it was not until 1628 that the writs for elections began to be executed in the names of the inhabitants and burgesses of Aylesbury. Henceforth Aylesbury would have the distinction of being a parliamentary borough, but not a corporate one.

Meanwhile, beginning around 1550, another protracted dispute had arisen over the estate left to the town by John Bedford in 1494 for the twin objectives of repairing the roads and relieving the poor of Aylesbury, which was in danger of being lost by neglect and sharp practice. It proved necessary to go to the expense of procuring a private Act of Parliament, passed in 1597. It is still the governing instrument of the (unfortunately much diminished) charity. The Act created a different sort of corporation, the Incorporated Surveyors of the Highways of Aylesbury, to manage the affairs of the charity. Of the nine so-called

41 *Royal visit, 1603. Soon after his accession in 1603 James I visited Aylesbury with a large entourage as the guest of Sir John Pakington, lord of the manor. These fragments of wall paintings incorporating loyal sentiments were later uncovered in the* Crown *inn, a Pakington property.*

'feoffees' named, one, Thomas Fountain (of Walton), is styled gentleman and the rest are described as yeomen. The latter title is not a strictly accurate description of most of the nine, who were largely tenant farmers, but it is indicative of the role of agriculture in the economy of the town in this period.

Sir Thomas Pakington died in 1571 and was buried in Aylesbury with pomp and ceremony. Under his will Aylesbury passed first to his widow, Dorothy, who married Thomas Tasborough, a local squire, in 1575, and then to his son John, who was knighted in 1567. Sir John Pakington was a noted courtier and a royal favourite whose extravagant lifestyle led him into debt and a subsequent period of enforced retrenchment, from which he was eventually rescued by marriage to a wealthy widow in 1598. Although he built himself a mansion at Westwood near Droitwich, he is said to have resided chiefly at Aylesbury. Shortage of cash would explain his selling off of a large number of estate properties between 1577 and the 1590s, many of them to the existing tenants holding for fixed

rents. He is said to have enclosed Haydon Hill around 1600 and he also disposed of a substantial property at Stocklake to the non-resident Farmer family. Shortly after the accession of James I in 1603 Sir John had the doubtful honour of entertaining the new king, together with his queen and a large retinue, at Aylesbury. It must have been a very splendid (and expensive) occasion.

An incomplete manorial survey of 1602 shows evidence of further settlement growth, mostly in the form of infilling, since 1500. Among the streets, lanes and rows, mentioned by name are Balky's Lane (Cambridge Street), Church Way, Silver Street, Silver Lane, Butchers Row, Bakers Row, Cordwainers Row and Tanners alias Drapers Row. Situated in, or near, Butchers Row were two slaughter houses, a scalding house, a candle house and a 'stock house', all structures connected with 'while-you-wait' meat processing, but only seven 'shops' as such are specified. There were now no fewer than seven inns: the *George*, the *Bell* and the *White Hart* (adjacent to the gaol and the 'gaol pit') in the market place and the *Swan*, the *Angel*, the *Lion* and the *Bull* in Kingsbury. Also mentioned is 'Behind Church', an area in the vicinity of White Hill on the north-west fringe of the town, in later times the abode of poor cottagers, probably indicating recent immigration from the countryside. The growing problems of widespread poverty and vagrancy had been the subject of recent national legislation culminating in the Poor Law Act of 1601, which provided for compulsory parish rates for the relief of the destitute.

Some confirmation that the Act was being heeded is found in an undated contemporary list of manorial 'ordinances for the town' which forbids the taking in of 'inmates' and orders the expulsion of seven named individuals (one of them an Irishman). Other ordinances concentrate largely on street cleaning, sanitation and the prevention of obstructions such as wood piles and dunghills. Drinking water is not to be fetched in carts but to be purchased from the common water carrier, carried on horseback in leather buckets. Officers appointed include, in addition to the constable, an ale taster, a flesh taster and two searchers and sealers of leather.

Sir John Pakington died in January 1625, aged 77 years, and was buried in Aylesbury. His only son, Sir John, 1st Baronet, born in 1600, had predeceased him the previous October. The entry of the latter's burial in the Aylesbury parish register describes him as 'knight and baronet, the hopes of Aylesbury', a sentiment which suggests that relations between town and family may have softened over the years. Young John left an infant son, another John, born in 1620, who was thus heir to the family estates. The Aylesbury manor house remained in the occupation of the 1st Baronet's widow.

The period which culminated in the English Civil War was one in which Buckinghamshire played a more prominent part in national politics than at any other time in its history. Yet while various forms of religious dissent had clearly taken root in parts of the Chilterns by the early 17th century, there is little evidence of overt disaffection in the town or of the kind of open contempt for the Church of England displayed by Puritans at Beaconsfield and elsewhere. Parish rates were levied for the repair of the church in 1632, 1637 and 1640. The chancel was repaired in 1628 at the expense of the Lee family of Quarrendon, who as lessees of the Prebendal manor, were responsible for its upkeep. Sir Henry Lee

42 *Monument to Lady Anne Lee (d. 1590), wife of Sir Henry Lee of Quarrendon, and her children in the parish church.*

43 *Statue of John Hampden (1494-1643), Buckinghamshire squire and Parliamentary leader, in Aylesbury market place, where he mustered the local militia on the eve of the Civil War. He raised his own regiment of infantry and died at Thame in 1643 from injuries sustained at the battle of Chalgrove Field.*

was also the founder, in 1598, of a modestly endowed grammar school located near the church about which little is known at this time.

Buckinghamshire provided the focus of resistance to the attempt of Charles I to levy the Ship Money tax without the consent of Parliament, which had been dissolved in 1629. John Hampden of Great Hampden, a local squire whose statue now stands in Market Square, refused to pay the tax and in 1637 contested its legality. The verdict in the great Ship Money trial went against him, but he had helped to set in motion a series of events which led eventually to Civil War. It was at the county town of Aylesbury in June 1642 that John Hampden and Arthur Goodwin of Wooburn mustered the county militia, obedient to an ordinance of the Long Parliament and in defiance of the king's command, an action that was tantamount to open rebellion. The following August the King's standard was raised at Nottingham: the Civil War had begun. Aylesbury's lord, the youthful Sir John Pakington, lost little time in joining the royalist army. Only one other Aylesburian is known to have followed his example.

Owing to its strategic situation, a mere twenty-odd miles from Oxford, which became the King's headquarters until 1646, and commanding as it did one of the approaches to London, Aylesbury was early fortified with earthen ramparts and defended by a large garrison, first of militiamen and then of regular soldiers under the command of a series of military governors. For some time it was the only such garrison in the county and it remained for the duration of the war the most important centre of

44   *Early 17th-century spur found near Aylesbury. It shows signs of having been gilt.*

45   *Iron left-hand dagger, 16th-17th century, from Aylesbury.*

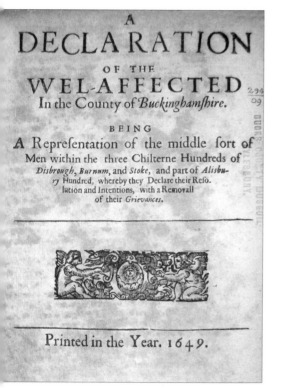

A

DECLARATION

OF THE

WEL-AFFECTED

In the County of *Buckinghamſhire*.

BEING

A Repreſentation of the middle ſort of Men within the three Chilterne Hundreds of *Disbrough*, *Burnum*, and *Stoke*, and part of *Alisbu-ry* Hundred, whereby they Declare their Reſo-lution and Intentions, with a Removall of their *Grievances*.

Printed in the Year. 1649.

Good and Joyfull Nevves

OVT OF

BVCKINGHAMSHIRE,

Being an exact and true Relation of a Battell, ſtricken betwixt Prince *ROBERT* and Sir *William Balfore*;

Lievtenant Generall to his Excellency, the Earle of *Eſſex*, neer *Alisbury* in that County on *Tueſday* laſt, the firſt of *November*, wherein the ſaid Sir *William* obtain'd a happy and glorious Victory.

London, Printed for *Francis Wright*, 1642.

46   *Throughout the Civil War Aylesbury was a Par-liamentary garrison protected by makeshift defences. In the Interregnum which followed discontent with the existing social order came to the surface and sects holding egalitarian opinions, including Anabaptists, Diggers and Levellers, found widespread support locally, as this 1649 pamphlet indicates.*

47   *Civil War pamphlet giving news of a successful Parliamentary encounter with a royalist force commanded by Prince Rupert ('Robert') near Ayles-bury on 1 November 1642, within days of the latter's victory at Edgehill.*

48   *Medal, found locally, depicting Robert Devereux, Earl of Essex, appointed Lord General by Parliament in 1642, who in June 1643 was briefly based at Thame preparatory to an abortive attack on Oxford. Obverse: portrait of the Earl within a laurel wreath inscribed in Latin 'For religion, law, king and parliament'. Reverse: the king in Parliament.*

military operations in mid-Buckinghamshire. There was constant skirmishing and foraging towards Oxford and Brill, a royalist outpost, and the town was under threat of attack more than once. It was even briefly occupied by royalist cavalry. Men from the Aylesbury garrison frequently served outside the county; they took part in the skirmish at Kineton in the aftermath of the battle of Edgehill in October 1642, in which Sir Edmund Verney of Claydon, the royalist standard-bearer, was killed. Sir John Pakington also took part in the battle on the royalist side. Cromwell visited the town more than once, halting there on his victorious return to London after the Battle of Worcester in September 1651 to receive a delegation of MPs.

Not a lot is known about the Aylesbury garrison, but Newport Pagnell, another strategic town in north Buckinghamshire which came under Parliamentary control in late 1643 and was promptly fortified, is better documented. The amount budgeted for the cost of the – admittedly state-of-the-art – defences there was £1,000 and 12,000 troops were assigned to the garrison. The Aylesbury garrison may well have been much smaller than this but it is likely to have far exceeded the number of inhabitants. At Aylesbury, money for making the fortifications was lent by two of the inhabitants, Joseph Saxton, innkeeper

at the *George*, and Richard Heywood. To make way for the walls numerous houses had to be demolished. Also demolished was the Pakington family's manor house; it was never rebuilt.

Leaving aside the threat of enemy action, the inhabitants would have had to endure such hardships as the quartering of soldiers, discipline, mutinies, disruption of agriculture, food shortages, requisitions and taxes. One effect of the experience was the emergence of a much greater intensity and diversity of religious opinion and practice in the town. At the very outset of the conflict a pulpit was erected in the market square from which to preach to the soldiers, debate and discussion about religion apparently being normal in the army. It is thus hardly surprising that well before the Restoration the Presbyterians, Baptists and other dissenting sects had acquired a considerable following in the area. One of the more prominent of the Baptists was Stephen Dagnall, a bookseller who published several pamphlets in which he expressed sympathy with the radical ideas of the Levellers.

During the war, and for a time after the garrison was disbanded and the fortifications demolished in July 1646, the county was administered by the Committee for Buckinghamshire appointed under a parliamentary ordinance of 1642. The

Committee met in the *George* inn in Aylesbury and was in virtually continuous session. Nominally it was quite a large body, incorporating men of local standing from all over Buckinghamshire. In practice its day-to-day business came to be dominated by a nucleus of five or six obscure individuals of relatively low social status, some of whom resided in or near Aylesbury. Prominent among them were Christopher Henn, a grazier who had formerly leased the Haydon Hill pasture, and Christopher Eggleton, a lawyer and

49 *Certificate to the Committee of Parliament for the Army concerning arrears of pay due to Sergeant-Major Christopher Eggleton, of Ellesborough near Aylesbury, for his service in the parliamentary army between 1643 and 1646. He was a member of the Committee for Buckinghamshire and was steward of the sequestered Pakington estates.*

small landowner from Ellesborough, near Wendover. Numerous other government agents and officials were also based in the town.

These men exercised a great deal of power and influence in military and religious matters and also in administering the confiscated and sequestrated estates of royalist 'malignants' throughout the county. They were often at odds with the military governor. In Aylesbury, following the effective abolition of episcopacy, the two prebendal estates were sold off in 1650 (the manor house of Walton having been destroyed during the war). The Aylesbury prebend was acquired by Thomas Scot, the regicide, who came from Marlow and was a member of the County Committee. He was elected MP for Aylesbury in 1645, together with Simon Mayne, landowner, of Dinton, another regicide.

For the people of Aylesbury the outcome of the war provided an opportunity to obtain redress for old grievances. Because Sir John Pakington had taken up arms against Parliament his estates had been sequestered and were redeemed in 1649 only on payment of a crippling fine following a period of imprisonment. A petition addressed to the House of Commons and signed by 87 inhabitants of Aylesbury, headed by Mathew Cockman, a Presbyterian whose family had earlier been bailiffs of the manor, set out the misdeeds of the Pakington family. It deprived them of their right of pasture at Haydon Hill and prevented them from making use of their 1554 charter of incorporation. It went on to refer to the great losses suffered by them 'by quartering of soldiers and pulling down their houses, digging up their orchards and fences to make way for the fortifications to the value of near £5,000', and asked the House as a mark of favour to settle upon them the benefit of common which they

50   *Page from the first volume of accounts of the overseers of the poor showing entries for the year 1657.*

formerly enjoyed and allow them to make 'such use of their charter of incorporation as may be most for the good of the said town', and assign to them 'the royalty of the town held of the crown' in the manner thought best.

The response of the Commons was to order the Committee for Compounding with Delinquents to settle the estate in question (i.e. Haydon Hill, comprising just under 153 acres), valued at £190 per annum by Pakington, on the inhabitants of Aylesbury, allowing Pakington in return an abatement of £2,670 on his fine. This order was duly given effect by a conveyance of January 1650 by which Pakington assigned to 13 feoffees (i.e. trustees) acting on behalf of the townspeople the pasture ground called Haydon Hill and also the waste ground of

the manor and the court leet within the area of the borough. It was also agreed that in future the steward of the court leet should be nominated jointly by Pakington and the town and that 'neither Sir John Pakington nor the town were to have absolute power the one over the other'.

Although the town's charter was not restored, despite another petition to Parliament, the 'Feoffees for Haydon Hill' evidently played a role in town government and may even in practice have exercised some degree of control over matters relating to poor relief, for a memorandum of 1657 in the overseers' account book states that the 'town stock' had been lent on bond to certain poor tradesmen by order of the feoffees, who were still in being as late as 1663.

Five

THE POST-RESTORATION PERIOD, 1660-1714

The Restoration of Charles II in 1660 brought many changes, both nationally and locally, most notably the re-establishment of the Church of England. In Aylesbury John Barton, the vicar who had been ejected in 1645 and had found refuge as chaplain to the Grenville family of Wotton Underwood, was reinstated and the intruded vicar, John Luff, was ejected. Church discipline was restored and action was taken against those who refused to attend the parish church. The lands belonging to the two prebends and the rights of the prebendaries were alike reclaimed. The general pardon granted by Charles II was not extended to the regicide Thomas Scott, who was executed at Charing Cross in October 1660. On the scaffold he boldly declared that God had engaged him in a cause that was 'not to be repented of'.

Sir John Pakington, 2nd Baronet (d. 1680), took advantage of the changed circumstances to seek the return of the Haydon Hill pasture and of his manorial rights on the grounds that the 1650 agreement had been made by him under duress; he eventually succeeded in his claim in 1664, by means of an Act of Parliament which was opposed on behalf of the inhabitants. The Restoration also saw the replacement of existing county justices of the peace by new ones, mostly drawn from the local landed gentry, as had been customary before the wars. But some changes caused by the war proved permanent. Although the Pakingtons continued to be lords of the manor for over a century they were henceforth absentee landlords residing at their family seat in Worcestershire. In the aftermath of the Restoration, too, Sir John found it necessary to sell off the *King's Head* and the *Crown* inn as well as the enclosed pasture called the Friarage, the site of the former manor house. Aylesbury was now a town without a resident squire.

The 1660s inaugurated a period of increasing prosperity for market towns generally, especially for towns such as Aylesbury situated on through-routes adapted for an expanding network of public wheeled transport. The evidence of the parish registers indicates that, despite an outbreak of plague in 1665, there was a gradual rise in the population after 1660 to around the 2,000 mark, the figure estimated in 1709. However, since burials usually exceeded baptisms, growth seems to have depended to a considerable extent on inward migration, much of it unwanted. We hear of cottages being erected on waste ground at Common Dunghill (in lower Castle Street) and Baker's Lane (Cambridge Street) end on the outskirts of the town.

51   *Late 17th-century weathercock of St Mary's church after re-gilding in the 1980s.*

A traveller who visited the town in 1702 described it in the following terms:

> ... hath a good market... for provisions: it is a pretty large town containing about 400 houses, the buildings of which are but indifferent; mostly timber but there are some tolerable houses in it, and 2 or 3 pretty good inns; it is also a post town and hath carriers and a stage coach goes every day to and from thence to London. It is the shire town where the assizes are generally kept; there is also the county gaol kept, and also at this town is the election for the knights of the shire made.

A later published directory of 1720 describes the rival town of Buckingham as the chief town of the county, but adds that 'Aylesbury is the most frequented and has the better trade' and is 'much better and cheaper than any other so near London'.

Yet prosperity remained out of reach of the majority of the inhabitants. The rate of exemptions from the Hearth Tax of 1662 seems to have been as high as 60 or 70 per cent and poverty remained a serious problem throughout the Restoration period and beyond. In 1681, for example, it was reported that when merchants raised the price of corn the poor women of Aylesbury and other nearby towns, including Buckingham and Winslow, attacked those that bought it.

It was the need for an increasing number of poor landless families, such as the squatters previously mentioned, to support themselves that provided the impetus for the development of cottage industries. By the early 1670s lace making was being taught to poor children in the care of the parish. In 1698 the number of poor persons living in Aylesbury 'which get their living by making of lace' was given in one source as 429, a very large number if even approximately accurate. Duck breeding, which, like lace making, was directed towards the London market, is not recorded in detail before 1750, but the place-name Duck End (apparently replacing Common Dunghill) is met with as early as the 1690s. Over time networks of dealers established themselves in both industries. Other new occupations at this time include bricklaying and brick making.

The relief of the destitute was the responsibility of the overseers of the poor and was financed by fortnightly collections. Their accounts, which begin in 1656, show that it took many different forms including regular cash doles, the boarding out of children, the provision of clothing and the maintenance of almshouses. As time went on the scope of relief tended to expand. In the 1670s there are examples of payments to the bone setter and others for medical assistance both to paupers and to the families of able-bodied men and in 1672 two children were sent to London to be touched by Charles II for the King's Evil, a distinctively royalist, or Tory, form of therapy.

Some insight into the commercial life of the town in this period is afforded by surviving trade tokens, mostly issued

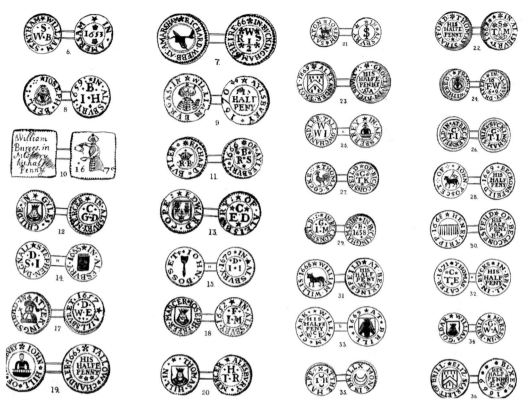

52   Trade tokens. In the 1650s and 1660s a chronic shortage of coinage led a great many tradesmen to issue their own token coins, usually giving the issuer's name and indicating the trade. Some 17 examples are recorded for Aylesbury. They include such sophisticated trades as coffee house keeper and bookseller.

between 1656 and 1670 to meet a chronic shortage of small change. There were in all 16 'tokeners', the highest total for any of the Buckinghamshire towns except Wycombe, which has twenty. The trades identified are innkeepers (three, at the Crown and King's Head), mercers and drapers (five), grocers and tallow chandlers (four), brewer, stationer, coffee house proprietor (Turk's Head). Coffee houses were a new and significant phenomenon. They acted as centres of information about politics and other matters by providing pamphlets, newspapers and other ephemeral reading matter.

The professions were represented locally chiefly by lawyers and one or two medical practitioners. The lawyers (including ecclesiastical lawyers) and physicians, together with the more prosperous farmers and innkeepers, constituted the elite of the town, apart from the occasional resident gentleman of independent means. Two notable examples of the latter were Thomas Farrer, JP, the lessee of the prebendal manor of Walton who died in 1703, and Francis Ligo, JP, whose family owned property in Stoke Mandeville but who chose to live in Aylesbury at this time. As justices of the peace, they were government appointees.

Not included in the list of trade tokens was the White Hart inn, whose facilities for travellers and visitors were greatly enhanced in 1663 by the addition of the Rochester Room, a free-standing rear extension to the White Hart, said to have

53 *Garden front of the former* White Hart *inn in Market Square by Nick Carter from an old photograph. This part of the building is said to have been built by the Earl of Rochester in 1663 as a offering of thanks to the then innkeeper for enabling him to evade capture during the Civil War period. The inn was demolished in 1864 to make way for the corn exchange.*

54 *The spacious (42ft x 23ft) Rochester Room was the scene of this notable equestrian feat in 1851. The print incidentally also gives an impression of the elaborate 17th-century decorative paintings and panelling.*

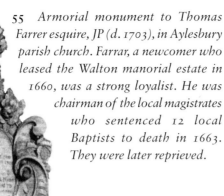

55 *Armorial monument to Thomas Farrer esquire, JP (d. 1703), in Aylesbury parish church. Farrar, a newcomer who leased the Walton manorial estate in 1660, was a strong loyalist. He was chairman of the local magistrates who sentenced 12 local Baptists to death in 1663. They were later reprieved.*

56 *Dagnall family monument. Matthias Dagnall (1658-1736), bookseller, who heads the list, was the son of Stephen, a pamphleteer, one of the 12 Baptists condemned by Thomas Farrar in 1663.*

been erected by the Earl of Rochester, who as a royalist fugitive during the Civil War had been helped to make his escape from the town by the then innkeeper. Spacious and elegant, it provided a substitute for the formal public assembly rooms provided for the entertainment of fashionable society in many towns after 1700. Generally, however, Aylesbury, although increasingly a place of resort in the late 17th century, especially during the twice-yearly assizes and at quarter sessions and county elections, was still deficient in many of the civilised amenities of town life calculated to induce people of wealth and fashion to actually take up residence there in any numbers.

A permanent legacy of the Civil War period was religious dissent. In the immediate aftermath of the Restoration, persecution of those refusing to attend their parish church was carried on by Church and state alike, though increasingly by the latter. It was at its most intense in the 1660s and flared up again in the 1680s. At a special episcopal visitation in 1662,

21 Aylesbury inhabitants were presented for 'contemptuously' absenting themselves from church. They included Stephen Dagnall, the Baptist bookseller and pamphleteer, Thomas Hill, a linen draper, and Richard Dalby, a schoolmaster. In 1663 a crisis arose when Dagnall, Hill and nine other local Baptists were proceeded against by the local magistrates under a semi-obsolete law of 1593 and were all sentenced to death. They were saved by a direct appeal to Charles II, who granted them all a reprieve and later a pardon. It was the only case of its kind in the whole country.

Nevertheless, the numbers of open Dissenters in Aylesbury appears to have gradually declined in the decades following 1660. In 1676 the so-called Compton Census gave a total of only 45 nonconformists as against 887 conformists, less than five per cent of the total. But a great many of those who conformed undoubtedly retained puritan sympathies and some were probably occasional conformists only. The Presbyterians, Baptists and Quakers all had

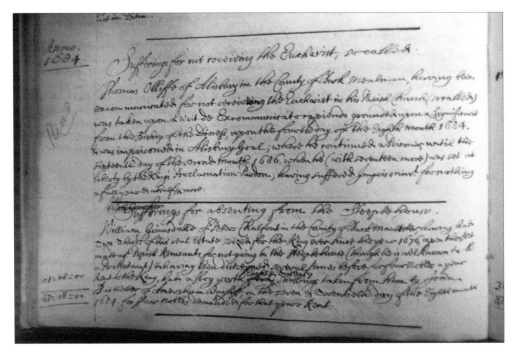

57 *Quaker 'Book of Sufferings'. A lasting legacy of the Civil War period was nonconformity in religion. Failure to comply with the norms of the Established Church was subject to severe legal penalties which fell particularly heavily on the Society of Friends, or Quakers, as witnessed in this record kept by the Aylesbury Friends.*

58 *Friends' meeting house, Rickfords Hill. The Quaker meeting house was first registered in 1703 under the Toleration Act of 1669. The present building dates from 1727.*

meeting houses in 1706. Such differences in religious sentiments gave a new edge to the fiercely partisan electoral politics which were a feature of the period.

Throughout virtually the whole of the reign of Charles II Aylesbury's two parliamentary seats were occupied by two neighbouring landowners, both former Roundheads and both moderates. They were Sir Thomas Lee (1635-91), baronet, of Hartwell and his step-father Sir Richard Ingoldsby, KB, of Dinton, the latter one of the regicides, a former colonel in the Parliamentary army and a close relation of Oliver Cromwell. By the 1670s, however, under the influence of Thomas Wharton (1648-1715), afterwards (1715) 1st Marquess of Wharton, the profligate son of the Puritan Philip, Lord Wharton (d. 1696), organised opposition to government was on the rise. Wharton, who was MP for Wendover from 1673 to 1679, and for the county from 1679-96, was a man of great wealth, with an estate at Wooburn in the Chilterns and another at Over Winchendon, close to Aylesbury, which he made his principal residence. His unparalleled talents as a political manager (he was said to know all the electors' children by name) would make him the acknowledged national leader of what would soon come to be known as the Whig party.

But the Whigs did not have things all their own way at Aylesbury. In 1679, in the midst of the intense excitement generated by the Exclusion Crisis, caused by the attempt to debar Charles II's Catholic brother, James, Duke of York, from the succession to the crown, the town had its first contested election, in which the candidates of the Tories (the new nickname for the 'Church and King' loyalists), aided by the intervention of local government officials, came close to winning. In 1681,

too, a loyal address to Charles II, couched in obsequious terms, was allegedly signed by over 260 electors, and a similar address following a plot to kill the King in 1683 expressed detestation of 'fanatics'.

Six years later, in the election held on the accession of James II in 1685, Lee and Ingoldsby were ousted by two Tories after many voters had been disqualified, presumably by the four parish constables for the borough (the hamlet of Walton was outside the parliamentary borough), who were the official returning officers,

59 *The tone and content of this loyal address to James II on his accession in 1685 (1684, Old Style) from the 'principal and major part of the inhabitants' of Aylesbury epitomise the bitter factionalism that pervaded the political and social life of the town in this period.*

60   *Militia muster book, 1663. Maintenance of law and order depended ultimately on the militia, a locally based force of amateur soldiers who could be called out in an emergency. It was officered by members of the local landed gentry under the overall direction of the Lord Lieutenant of the county.*

61   *Thomas Wharton (1648-1715), 1st Marquess of Wharton (1715) of Wooburn and Over Winchendon, the greatest political manager of his day. In the Aylesbury election of 1701 his wealth and influence turned a dispute between Ashby, a Whig voter, and White, a parish constable and thus one of the returning officers, into a constitutional crisis.*

on the grounds that they were in receipt of alms from Bedford's Charity and thus, as paupers, disqualified from voting. The Whig candidates claimed that they had received six times as many votes as their opponents, but to no avail. The Tories followed up their victory by bringing a Chancery action against the trustees of Bedford's Charity – all staunch Whigs – accusing them of various election malpractices, but without success.

In 1688 James II tried to do a deal with the more moderate Dissenters by offering them a measure of legal toleration, but it was too late. James's leading opponents had invited over his son-in-law, William of Orange, who became King in 1689. Among the first to join William was Wharton, who was made Comptroller of the Household to the new monarch. As a result of the Glorious Revolution the royal prerogative was curtailed and the powers of Parliament increased. Protestant dissenters were granted limited freedom of worship under the Toleration Act of 1689, but remained subject to various civil disabilities, including in practice deprivation of the right to sit in Parliament (though not of the right to vote).

Between 1689 and 1714, and more particularly during the reign of Queen Anne (1702-14), when a Tory ministry was in office on more than one occasion, electoral politics were constantly at fever pitch and nowhere more so than in Aylesbury. The parties – the Whigs, who were hostile to royal influence and were favoured by the Dissenters, and the Tories, who were loyal to the Church of England and whose staunchest backers locally were the Anglican clergy and the personnel (mostly laymen) of the local church courts – were often fairly evenly matched. Frequent general elections following the Triennial Act of 1694, which restricted the duration

of a Parliament to three years, helped to keep the political pot constantly on the boil. In Aylesbury, leaving aside direct bribery and intimidation, which were commonplace, there were two principal issues: firstly, the nature of the borough franchise – confirmed by Parliament in 1696 as all the (male) inhabitants not receiving alms, but leaving the definition of alms open to interpretation – and, secondly, the exercise of control over the

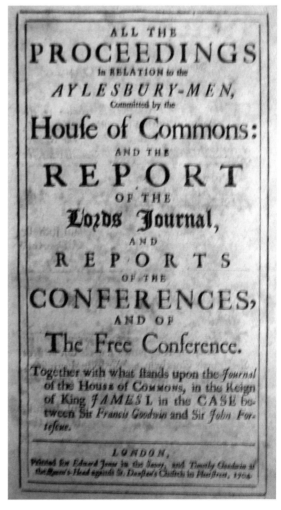

62   *Printed notice relating to* The Case of the Aylesbury Men. *This was the sequel to* Ashby v. White *in which Ashby was joined as plaintiff by five other poor voters.*

returning officers, namely the four elected parish constables, two of them elected for the principal manor and two for the prebendal.

It was this situation and its secret manipulation by Wharton (who succeeded to the earldom of Wharton in 1696 and, briefly, to the Lord Lieutenancy of the county in 1702) that produced the celebrated constitutional case known as *Ashby versus White* in 1701. Ashby, a licensed victualler, claimed to be a settled inhabitant of Aylesbury, and thus a voter, and White was one of the constables. On this occasion all four constables, whether Tories or not, had apparently agreed to reject Ashby's vote on the grounds that he had not gained a legal settlement in the town. With secret backing from Wharton's money and the assistance of Wharton's agent Robert Mead, a lawyer, Ashby brought a legal action against the constables. It was successful at the Buckinghamshire assizes but lost on appeal and was finally upheld by the House of Lords, where Wharton had a secure majority.

Five other Aylesbury men whose votes had also been rejected now took out writs in their turn. Then the House of Commons took exception to the Lords infringing their right to adjudicate on disputed elections and committed the plaintiffs and their lawyers (Robert Mead successfully evaded arrest) to prison for contempt. The little market town of Aylesbury had produced a constitutional crisis of the first magnitude which was only defused when Queen Anne decided to prorogue Parliament, thereby freeing the prisoners, but leaving the privileges of the Commons intact.

Six

GEORGIAN AYLESBURY, 1714-1836

After the Hanoverian succession in 1714 the pace of politics slackened, for the Whigs had managed to get their hands firmly on the levers of power and the Septennial Act of 1716 reduced the frequency of elections. Party politics did not disappear, but they became more complicated, especially where (as in Aylesbury) there were few or no Tory candidates at elections. Splits soon appeared in the Whig ranks between 'court' and 'country' Whigs, with the former sometimes making common cause with committed Tory voters, of whom there were still quite a few in Aylesbury. The death of the Marquess of Wharton in 1715 deprived the local Whigs of their leader, for his son and heir turned Jacobite and he had no real successor. The threat of rebellion was finally removed by the Battle of Culloden in 1745, an event preceded by panic in Aylesbury. As time went on elections became increasingly venal and outright bribery was increasingly employed as a means of securing votes.

The opening decades of the 18th century brought increasing prosperity and a quickening in the pace of change. Improvements included a partial piped water supply (the first of several such experiments) and a generously enlarged and endowed free grammar school near the church, erected in 1718-20 to replace the existing one. The grammar school owed its re-endowment to Henry Phillips (1640-1714) of London, son of a former MP for Aylesbury, whose cousin and executor William Mead, a retired London merchant, oversaw its construction. Despite its name, the great majority of the boys attending the grammar school were taught reading and writing only. The building now forms part of the County Museum and Art Gallery.

From 1720 it became the practice to hold the summer assizes at Buckingham and the winter assizes at Aylesbury and in 1747 Buckingham's political patrons succeeded in having the arrangement confirmed by Act of Parliament, a situation which survived for a century. The dispute over Buckingham's claim to be the county town had apparently been exacerbated by the decision in 1720 to rebuild the ancient county gaol and court house in Aylesbury. By 1722 work had begun, but in 1724 the money ran out and legal difficulties were raised about levying further rates for the purpose. As a result the present handsome brick County Hall (the gaol buildings, which housed both felons and debtors, were at the rear, on a long narrow site extending to the brook) was not finally completed until 1740. Like the assizes, the gaol made an important contribution to the town's economy, but outbreaks of gaol fever were

63   *The newly fashionable brick front of the old Grammar School of c.1718-20, seen from the churchyard. It now forms part of the County Museum.*

64   *The County, or Shire, Hall in Market Square; begun in 1722. Problems of finance delayed completion until 1737. The ground-floor window on the left side was originally the entrance to the former gaol at the rear of the building. The entrance to the upstairs courtroom is on the right.*

65 *(Right) Contemporary drawing of the treadmill erected in the county gaol in the early 19th century to provide hard labour for prisoners. It was used to grind corn and pump water, but accidents, often fatal, were common. It was condemned in 1841 by the Inspectors of Prisons, who also reported unfavourably on the gaol as a whole.*

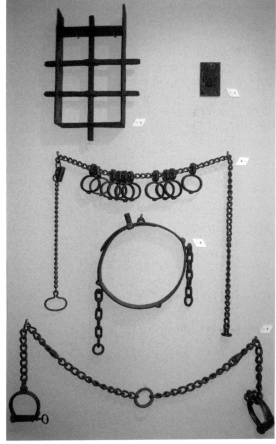

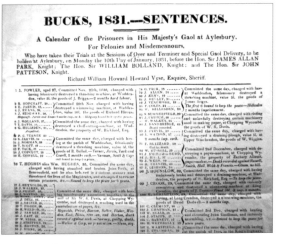

66 *Calendar of prisoners, with their sentences, January 1831.*

67 *Plaque on boundary wall of old gaol.*

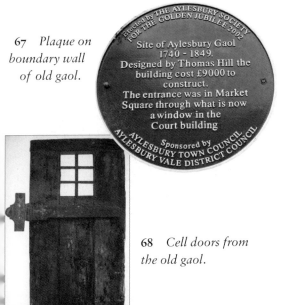

68 *Cell doors from the old gaol.*

69 *(Right) Restraining irons from the old gaol.*

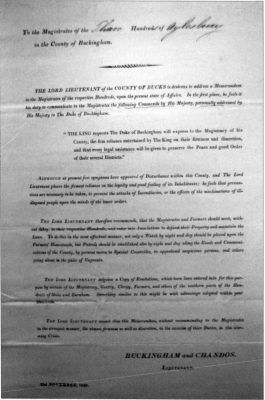

WHEREAS several evil-minded Persons did, on *Wednesday, March* the 14th, 1770, about One o'Clock in the Morning, with Force of Arms, break into his Majesty's Goal at *Aylesbury*, in the County of *Bucks*, and thereby relieved two Prisoners under Sentence of Death: The Keeper of the said Goal does hereby promise a Reward of TEN POUNDS to any Person that shall apprehend and secure either of the said Prisoners, and give Notice thereof to Mr THOMAS SMITH, Keeper of the said Goal.

Edward Berry, convicted of Burglary, by Trade a Baker, lately resided in and about London, about five Feet six Inches high, with very dark-brown Hair inclining to curl, pitted with the Small-Pox, a pale Complexion, thin-visaged, a little Rising on his Nose; had on when he went away a dark-brown Beaver-Fur Coat, a Thickset Frock and Waistcoat, a greasy Pair of Leather Breeches, Silver Knee-Buckles, and Black Stockings.

John Turner, convicted for returning from Transportation, born at *Aylesbury*, by Trade a Butcher, is a well-set Man, about five feet seven Inches high, wore his own Hair strait and dark-brown, full and fresh faced, a large Roman Nose, has a downcast Look; had on when he went away a light-colour'd Fustian Frock and Waistcoat lined with Shalloon, and a pair of greasy Leather Breeches.

N. B. The above Prisoners were double iron'd, and escaped with their Irons.

70   *Reward notice for escaped prisoners awaiting execution, 1770.*

71   *Circular dated November 1830 from the Lord Lieutenant to magistrates and farmers asking for precautions to be taken to protect property against disturbances among 'the lower orders'. The reference is to the so-called Swing riots, the result of widespread unemployment among agricultural workers and manifested in Buckinghamshire by scattered outbreaks of machine-breaking in several parts of the county in October 1830.*

72   *Print of a trial in progress in the 18th-century courtroom (early 19th century).*

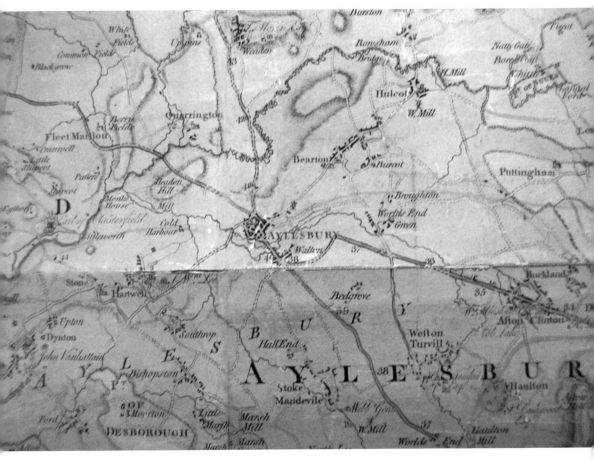

73 *Extract from Thomas Jeffreys' map of Buckinghamshire, surveyed 1766-8 and engraved 1768, showing Aylesbury and its immediate vicinity.*

not uncommon and represented a threat to the inhabitants at large.

Both grammar school and court house were built of local brick, as were many other buildings, public and private, in this period so that the town was gradually taking on a new and more symmetrical appearance than that which it had presented to the visitor of 1702. This was because brick had become fashionable. Some – even among the well-to-do – contented themselves with re-fronting their timber-framed houses in brick. William Mead, the builder of the grammar school, was also responsible for rebuilding the Prebendal House, originally in the contemporary Queen Anne style,

but since modified. Other examples of larger town houses of this period in brick include the present Barclays Bank in Market Square, formerly part of the endowment of Bedford's Charity, and No. 1 Church Street (re-fronted in 1739), once the home of Thomas Hickman (d. 1698), a writing master and the founder of the almshouses charity that still bears his name. It was afterwards the residence of the Williams family, a dynasty of apothecaries. Green End House in Rickford Hill was built in brick around 1700 and later re-fronted in stucco.

By far the best known of the occupants of the Prebendal House was the youthful

74 *Aylesbury from the west, c.1738. This distant view of the town is a detail from one of a series of paintings of the new gardens at Hartwell House by the Spanish artist Balthazar Nebot. The parish church dominates the skyline on the left and the new Shire Hall is on the right.*

John Wilkes (1727-97), whose later political career was to win him national celebrity and notoriety in almost equal measure. Wilkes, who had spent some of his education in Aylesbury, acquired the Prebendal through his estranged wife, Mary Mead, whom he married in 1747. She had inherited the lease from her uncle William Mead. The son of a London distiller, Wilkes had been educated as a gentleman and his new residence, suitably enhanced, gave him status locally. The lordship of the prebendal manor gave him control of two of the

returning officers and encouraged him to seek election to Parliament. In the event, however, Wilkes found himself forced to pay out huge sums in bribes to his poorer constituents. Although he was eventually

75 *Memorial to Sir Francis Bernard in the parish church of St Mary. One of the Bernards of Nether Winchendon, he was the last governor of the Massachusets Bay colony. Soon after his return from America in 1769 he settled at the Prebendal House, where he died in 1779. There is a separate memorial to his wife (d. 1778).*

IN
MEMORY
OF SIR FRA.ˢ BERNARD BARᵗ
LATE GOV.ᴿ OF MASSACHUSETS BAY
HE MARRIED
AMELIA DAUᵗ OF STEPHEN OFFLEY ESQ.
OF NORTON HALL DERBYSHIRE
BY WHOM HE LEFT ISSUE
THREE SONS
IOHN, THOMAS, AND SCROPE,
AND FOUR DAUGHTERS
IANE, AMELIA, FRANCES ELIZ.ᵗᴴ
AND IULIA
HE DIED
THE XVIᵗᴴ DAY OF IUNE
M.DCC.LXXIX
IN THE LXVII YEAR
OF HIS AGE

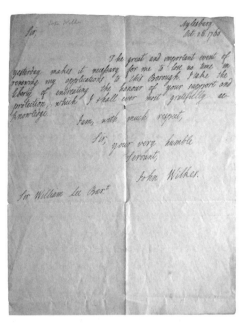

76   *Portrait print of John Wilkes, Aylesbury's most celebrated resident. He was MP for the borough from 1757 to January 1764.*

77   *Note from Wilkes to Sir William Lee of Hartwell, seeking his support in the impending general election occasioned by the death of George II, October 1760.*

78   *The Prebendal House was formerly the manor house of a small estate, the endowment of a prebend, or canonry, in the cathedral church of Lincoln. The present house, built in the early 18th century, was extensively remodelled by John Wilkes in the 1750s. The two-storey front bays are an early 19th-century addition.*

elected in a by-election in 1757 and was unopposed in the 1761 general election, by 1763, disillusioned and heavily in debt, he had quit Aylesbury forever. His successor at the Prebendal House was Sir Francis Bernard of Nether Winchendon, Buckinghamshire, the last governor of the Massachusets Bay colony, who leased the house from Sir William Lee of Hartwell House and moved in with his family in 1772, a refugee from the tedium of rural life. He died there in 1779.

During this period the coaching trade, which had burgeoned in the late 17th century, was benefiting from the new turnpike roads which were gradually spreading out in all directions from the capital. These were run by individual trusts authorised by private Acts of Parliament to charge tolls to finance the provision of better road surfaces and other improvements. The first to affect Aylesbury directly was the Wendover-Buckingham turnpike on the line of the present A413, established in 1721. The Sparrowsherne turnpike on

the A41 followed in 1762 and by 1810 the town was ringed around with tollgates. Improved roads brought increased traffic and faster vehicles; by the 1790s there were daily public stagecoaches from Aylesbury to London, Birmingham and Banbury and numerous stage waggons. Better roads helped bring town and countryside together. Between 1742 and the mid-1780s horse races, accompanied by dances and other entertainments, were held annually at Haydon Hill where the gentry from all over the county mingled with the more respectable citizens of Aylesbury.

This was the heyday of the coaching inn, of which the former *White Hart* at the bottom of the market place, with its spacious accommodation (including a ballroom), its extensive stabling and its bowling green, was Aylesbury's finest example. Its amenities even included its own pew in the parish church. The other principal inns were the *King's Head, George, Crown, Bull's Head, Bell, Red Lyon* and *Black Swan*. A total of 39 licensed victuallers

79 *Earthenware mug with embossed motif of an angel holding a palm leaf and a crown and inscribed with the name of Thomas Towers, who was licensee of the* George *inn in the 1750s. It stood on the north side of the market place and was the highest-rated of Aylesbury's licensed premises at the relevant time. It was pulled down in 1936.*

80 *A female politician. Portrait print of Pat (Martha in the burial register) Alexander. According to Gibbs, she kept the 'old'* Green Man *public house in Market Square. She is shown with a copy of* The Craftsman, *an anti-Whig journal founded in 1726. The serial number, if correct, dates it to 1735. She died in 1741 aged 85.*

81 *Quarrendon chapel in 1817. As a result of the conversion of arable to pasture in the 16th century the adjoining village of Quarrendon gradually became depopulated. By 1817 only the abandoned medieval church remained. Now only a portion of the north aisle is visible above ground.*

of all types was registered in 1753. One result of the availability of inns and other lodging places was that, like other market towns, Aylesbury was regularly home to a considerable number of soldiers who were billeted there for long periods in the virtual absence of military barracks. Though not always popular, they helped to provide trade for the local shopkeepers. Many married local girls, while a few, not exclusively the officers, brought their wives with them.

Agriculture remained the basis of the economy of the whole area. It was also the greatest single employer of labour in the town and parish of Aylesbury. Farmhouses were still located within the town itself or in Walton village and farms now ranged in size from under 30 acres to some 50 acres or more. Most of the larger farmers were tenants occupying family farms which were passed on from one generation to the next. Mixed arable farming seems to have predominated in the first half of the century, but later there was a trend towards conversion to pasture for grazing and dairying. William Harding, a bachelor who farmed some 150 acres of freehold land at Walton and its vicinity, left his property and cash (much of it acquired by money lending) to found an apprenticing charity in 1717.

The open, or common, fields of Aylesbury were enclosed by private Act of Parliament in 1771, while Walton hamlet had to wait a further 30 years until it too was enclosed in 1801. Both Acts made provision for the extinction of tithes payable to the Church. This was the origin of the Prebendal Farm, a totally new farm belonging to the prebendary of Aylesbury in Lincoln Cathedral in his capacity of rector. During the tenancy of J.K. Fowler (better

82   *Aylesbury Market House, 1806-66. It stood in the centre of the market place and was superseded by the new Corn Exchange.*

known as the landlord of the old *White Hart*) in the following century it would become the venue for steeplechasing. The vicar of Aylesbury also received a much smaller landholding in lieu of his 'small' tithes. By consolidating holdings, enclosure made it possible for new farmhouses to be erected in the fields but it proved to be a very gradual process.

Aylesbury's weekly market expanded greatly in the 18th century. In 1700 the tolls were being let at £25 a year; by 1757 this figure had risen to £94. In 1792 there were no fewer than six annual fairs, including one in October which doubled as a hiring fair. The increasing number and variety of retail shops was equally striking. A published directory of 1792, the earliest of its kind, lists nine specialist grocers and eight drapers, while the many other retailers included a stationer, brandy merchant, ironmonger and potash seller, as well as some who offered a wide variety

of wares. A high proportion of business operations were carried out on credit and some shopkeepers performed many of the functions of bankers.

The logical outcome of this was that one or two of the more successful wholesalers eventually became bankers in name as well as in fact. The first to do so was William Rickford (1730-1803), a grocer who, jointly with his son of the same name, founded the Aylesbury Old Bank, later (1853) the Oxon and Bucks and now Lloyds. Rickford's bank was soon rivalled by that of James Neale, a draper, who was in partnership with Robert Dell, a brandy merchant, and J.S. Woodcock, another draper, by 1802. The emergence of the two banks is indicative of the expansion of trade. Both drew on large London banks. As we shall see, the ramifications of their connections extended into politics. Neale's bank proved short-lived, for it was forced by financial difficulties to cease trading in 1813.

Consolidation was also taking place in other areas of life. In Aylesbury, unlike most larger towns, private brewing seems to have remained the rule until after 1750 and there were still six maltsters listed in 1792. But already, in 1786, Thomas Dell, maltster and brandy merchant, James Fell, lace dealer, and John Barker, farmer, all of Aylesbury, had formed a partnership as common brewers. And they were not quite the first, for Edward Terry, whose family would later be associated with the Aylesbury Brewery Company, was already in business with John Turvey. Other, mostly small-scale, manufacturing industries found in the town at this time included brick making, flour milling, basket making and leather crafts.

The other side of the picture was increased destitution among the growing mass of the unskilled working population, who comprised well over half of the total population of the town. Under the Elizabethan poor laws those unable to maintain themselves – principally widows, orphans and the aged – were entitled to assistance from the parish rates. In the later 17th century the overseers of the poor, who were the responsible parish officers, were employing a range of expedients, including regular maintenance payments, parish housing, subsidised rents, provision of work in the form of hemp-spinning or lacemaking, apprenticing of poor children, and the provision of clothing and medical assistance. But there are indications that attitudes were hardening in the face of increasing demand. By the early 1730s compulsory admission to a strictly regulated residential parish workhouse, run by a paid manager, was being enforced, though it was later relaxed. The ratepayers' burden was eased to some extent by parish charities including Bedford's, Hickman's almshouses (1698) and William Harding's apprenticing charity (1719), which put poor children in 'proper' trades with a preference for places other than Aylesbury. By 1751 the care of the poor and the workhouse were being contracted out for an annual payment of £400, excluding costs of removals (of non-parishioners) and cases of smallpox contracted outside the workhouse.

Contracting out, or 'farming', the poor by the year would seem to have become normal, though not invariable, but a new and stricter regime is indicated by a vestry resolution in 1758 that 'under no pretence whatever should the overseers pay or cause to be paid any sums of money for the relief of persons who refuse to come into the workhouse, and that ... no rent will be paid or allowed'. In following decades the situation became gradually worse, exacerbated by a rapidly rising population and by unemployment

and under-employment in agriculture. In 1783-5 the annual net expenses of the poor were put at almost £1,000. In 1795, a crisis year of inflation and scarcity following the outbreak of war with France, there were bread riots in Aylesbury, and the county magistrates were forced to sanction the subsidising of wages from the rates on the basis of need. In 1803 annual expenditure on the poor was returned at £2,053 in a total population of just over three thousand.

The long French war was brought even closer to the inhabitants of Aylesbury in 1807 when the exiled French king, Louis XVIII, and his numerous household were installed in nearby Hartwell House. Local tradesmen benefited from the greatly increased demand for provisions thereby generated and must have regretted Louis's

will be found.
⁎ The above SHOP to be Let, inquire of Mr. BIGGS, on the Premises.   (*One Property.*)

Singular Sale of Furniture.

TO BE SOLD BY AUCTION,
By Messrs. J. and R. GIBBS,

In a large Barn, on the Premises at HARTWELL HOUSE, (one mile from Aylesbury,) by order of the Rev. Sir G. Lee, Bart. on Wednesday the 13th of Sept., 1820, and two following days, precisely at eleven o'clock,

ABOUT Five Hundred LOTS of VALUABLE HOUSEHOLD FURNITURE, late the Property of his Majesty the King of France, and his Establishment; consisting of twelve capital Beds, seventy-six Wool and Hair Mattresses, seventy-eight Bedsteads, various, some with good Hangings; forty-eight Feather Bolsters, seventy-four pair Blankets, fifteen Chests of Drawers, eighty-eight Mahogany and other Dining, Card, and other Tables; sixteen large & small Glasses, one hundred and forty-six Elbow and other Chairs, various; three Mahogany Bookcases with Secretaires; nine Mahogany Chamber Cupboards and Stands; eleven Turkey and other Carpets; nine Mahogany and other Wardrobes; seven Clothes Presses; twenty-three Grates, various; one hundred dozen Wine Bottles; large Casks and Brewing Tubs, with many other valuable Effects.

Descriptive Catalogues of which may be had of the Game Keeper, on the Premises; at the principal Inns in every town within twenty miles, and of the Auctioneers, Aylesbury and Bicester.

FREEHOLD INN,

83 *Advertisement in the* Buckinghamshire, Bedfordshire and Hertfordshire Chronicle *of the sale of household furniture at Hartwell House, late the property of the King of France, September 1820.*

84   *Plaque in Bourbon Street re change of name in 1814.*

THE AYLESBURY SOCIETY
Erected by THE GOLDEN JUBILEE 2002
FOR THE

Bourbon Street
formerly known as
Waterhouse Street.
It was renamed in 1814 in
honour of Louis XVIII of
France who spent his exiled
years at nearby
Hartwell House

AYLESBURY TOWN COUNCIL
Sponsored by
AYLESBURY VALE DISTRICT COUNCIL

departure in April 1814. When the King's carriage processed through the town it was accompanied on its way by an entourage of members of the local Yeomanry Cavalry and others. This episode is commemorated by the name Bourbon Street, previously Waterhouse Street.

The situation of the Established Church in Aylesbury in the first half of the 18th century left a good deal to be desired. Although the parish church was a large and impressive edifice and its official congregation (i.e. all the inhabitants) numerous, the parish had been a vicarage since medieval times and as a result the living was poorly endowed, being valued at only £50 a year in 1710, well below the £80 considered by many to be the minimum desirable income of a vicar. This helps to explain why the two vicars who held office between 1729 and 1790 were non-resident pluralists whose places were supplied by a succession of ill-paid curates. Three of the curates in question – John Stephens, friend and dogsbody of John Wilkes, William Pugh and William Stockins – were also successive masters of the free grammar school, a more lucrative appointment than that of curate.

From 1790 resident vicars again became the rule, but not all of them, or their curates, were a credit to their cloth, and the state of the church at the close of the century was said by one contemporary to be very bad and getting worse. The situation improved with the appointment of John Morley, DD, who held office from 1816 to 1842. He was the author of several books and an active participant in local agitation against the slave trade. Yet even he, together with his wife and their 11 children, had to be rescued from acute financial difficulties by a huge public subscription in 1821. The parish church remained central to the

85   *Hartwell House near Aylesbury. It was the residence of the exiled Louis XVIII and his numerous retinue from c.1807 to April 1814.*

86   *South view of St Mary's parish church by T. Trotter (d. 1803), a mason. At this period, and later, the upper form of the nearby grammar school was accommodated in the church.*

87   *The elegant late 18th-century gateway to the churchyard at the Church Street entrance.*

religious and social life of the parish as a whole, but the building was reported to be in a dangerous structural state in 1765. Nothing much seems to have been done about it and Aylesbury may have been lucky to escape the fate of Buckingham, where the church tower collapsed in 1776. The two transepts were partitioned off and used for storage (the parish fire engine was kept there). The chancel, being the responsibility of the rector, was extensively repaired in the 1760s.

In some respects the condition of the body of the church reflected the social and economic distinctions of the community at large. The whole of the nave was filled with 'faculty' pews of all shapes and sizes, over which the well-to-do occupiers enjoyed exclusive rights. Some were fitted with brass rails and cloth hangings for greater privacy. Most impressive of all was the manorial pew, which was of the 'birdcage' type; normally accommodating the leading manorial tenants, at the assize sermon service it was reserved for the judges and the high sheriff. Additional seating was

provided by the erection of galleries. One was erected in 1756; another, a west gallery measuring over 20 feet in width, was put up around 1781 and paid for, according to one source, by 'the singers'; a third appeared in 1812.

The west gallery almost certainly accommodated the choir, for the singing of metrical psalms by 'west gallery' parish choirs had become widespread in the 18th century, both in town and country. They were commonly accompanied by a band of amateur instrumentalists, but in Aylesbury's case a reference to an organ, the gift of a parishioner in 1782, suggests otherwise. When Morley, by then in his seventies and recently remarried, introduced a new hymn book in 1833 the choir rebelled, parish opinion was polarised and a bitter dispute ensued which dragged on for years, involving petitions and counter-petitions to the Bishop of Lincoln and at least one lawsuit over the right of access to the organ loft.

The dissenting churches had undergone a relative decline locally after 1689, but

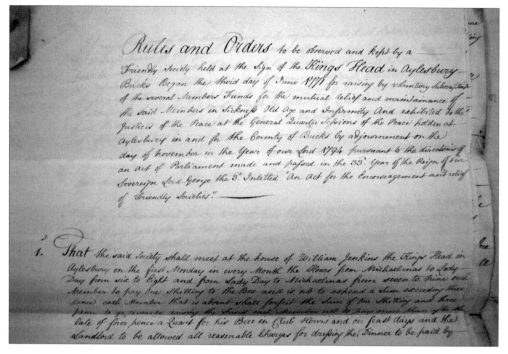

Rules and Orders to be observed and kept by a
Friendly Society held at the Sign of the Kings Head in Aylesbury
Bucks Began the third day of June 1771 for raising by voluntary Subscription
of the several Members Funds for the mutual relief and maintainance of
the said Members in Sickness Old Age and Infirmity And exhibited to the
Justices of the Peace at the General Quarter Sessions of the Peace holden at
Aylesbury in and for the County of Bucks by adjournment on the
day of November in the Year of our Lord 1794 pursuant to the directions of
an act of Parliament made and passed in the 33ʳᵈ Year of the Reign of our
Sovereign Lord George the 3ʳᵈ Intitled "An Act for the Encouragement and relief
of Friendly Societies".

1. That the said Society shall meet at the house of William Jenkins the Kings Head in
Aylesbury on the first Monday in every Month the Hours from Michaelmas to Lady
Day from six to Eight and from Lady Day to Michaelmas from seven to Nine each
Member to pay one shilling to the Box and is not to expend a Sum exceeding three
pence each Member that is absent shall forfeit the Sum of One Shilling and three
pence ...
late of four pence a Quart for his Beer in Club hours and on feast days and the
Landlord to be allowed all reasonable Charges for dressing the Dinner to be paid by

88 *Rules of the Friendly Society held at the* King's Head, *begun 1771 and registered at Quarter Sessions in 1794.*

this was about to change. The movement associated with the name of John Wesley, who preached in Wycombe in 1762, was slow to reach north Buckinghamshire. Under the leadership of James Durley, a Bierton carpenter, Wesleyan Methodism began to make steady progress in many of the surrounding villages after 1786, but it

89 *Aylesbury token coin, 1796. The obverse shows the head of William III with the legend 'To the Friends for the Abolition of Slavery' and the reverse the cap of liberty on a pole. Such local tokens were a response to a temporary scarcity of small change. The slave trade was just beginning to become a popular issue in the town at this date.*

was not until 1822 that the headship of the 'circuit' was transferred to Aylesbury, where the Castle Street chapel vacated by the Independents was taken over. Meanwhile, the wider religious revival touched off by Wesley was making itself felt even in the Established Church. In 1829 an official return to Quarter Sessions put the number of nonconformists in Aylesbury at around 600, including a solitary Quaker. Congregations were estimated as Independents 900; Methodists 500; Baptists 350. These figures are for adults and would include those attending from outside the parish. The Independents' most prominent member was John Rolls (1756-1837), a currier, or wholesaler in leather, who lived at Walton Grove and who was related to the prosperous families of Payne (also curriers) and Gibbs.

The wider social effects of the religious revival were becoming apparent by the 1820s. It contributed to a gradual reform of manners, or at any rate to the disappearance of the worst crudities and cruelties, one example being the suppression of public bull-baiting in the town after 1822. In politics, too, this decade signalled the beginnings of a new era when national issues – including slavery, Catholic emancipation and the legal disabilities of Dissenters – began to loom large locally. It also saw the growth of a separate and distinct dissenting political interest which was to be the driving force behind liberal and reforming movements from this time forward. It led to a good deal of friction with Anglican conservatives, but there was also much common ground on issues which had a strong appeal to the emerging middle classes generally.

By the end of the 18th century electoral politics in Aylesbury had reached new depths of corruption. A considerable proportion of the adult male population had come to rely on generous bribes at elections, particularly if contested, and regular 'sweeteners' in intervening years. But, though open to bribery, the voters cherished their independence of patron and by the late 1780s the growing influence and immense wealth of the Temple-Grenville family of Stowe, near Buckinham, threatened to turn Aylesbury into a proprietary borough. In 1789 their ally, Scrope Bernard of Nether Winchendon, landowner and banker, was elected for Aylesbury in a by-election and retained his seat in the general election of 1790. This was uncontested, but Bernard and the other candidate each gave presents of £7 and a guinea to their supporters.

At the general election of 1802 the mass of the electors wanted an outside candidate to 'up' the bidding. The opinions of the independent voters were more mixed. The Aylesbury bankers were at odds, for

William Rickford was at this time hand in glove with Bernard and the Grenvilles while Neale and Dell were on the other side. The upshot was that the appropriately named Robert Bent, a wealthy East India merchant, with James Neale as intermediary, was brought in as a third candidate and duly 'bought his way into the hearts of the electors' in traditional fashion. Bernard came third in the voting while a last-minute fourth candidate, T.F. Fremantle of Swanbourne, came bottom of the poll with only a handful of votes.

A petition was lodged against Bent's election on grounds of bribery and when it came before a Parliamentary Committee

ANNO QUADRAGESIMO QUARTO

GEORGII III. REGIS.

C A P. LX.

An Act for the preventing of Bribery and Corruption in the Election of Members to serve in Parliament for the Borough of *Aylesbury* in the County of *Buckingham*.   [29th *June* 1804.]

WHEREAS there was the most notorious Bribery and Corruption at the last Election of Burgesses to serve in Parliament for the Borough of *Aylesbury* in the County of *Buckingham*: And whereas such Bribery and Corruption is likely to continue and be practised in the said Borough in future, unless some Means are taken to prevent the same: In order, therefore, to prevent such unlawful Practices for the future, and that the said Borough may from henceforth be duly represented in Parliament; be it enacted by the King's most Excellent Majesty, by and with the Advice and Consent of the Lords Spiritual and Temporal, and Commons, in this present Parliament assembled, and by the Authority of the same, That from henceforth it shall and may be lawful to and for every Freeholder, being above the Age of Twenty-one Years, who shall have within the Three Hundreds of *Aylesbury*, or One or more of them, in the County of *Buckingham*, a Freehold of the clear yearly Value of Forty Shillings, to give his Vote at every Election of a Burgess or Burgesses to serve in Parliament for the said Borough of *Aylesbury*.

7 A   II. And

90 *Aylesbury Bribery Act, 1804. In Aylesbury householders not in receipt of alms were entitled to vote in parliamentary elections. They were notoriously venal. The Act sought to make the cost of general bribery prohibitive by greatly extending the borough boundaries for electoral purposes.*

in 1804 he was unseated. The petitioner was Fremantle, together with 10 others headed by the Rev. William Lloyd, vicar of Aylesbury, Robert Browne and Acton Chaplin. All four were closely associated with the Grenvilles: Fremantle, a naval officer, was a client of the Marquess of Buckingham; Browne was his tenant and dependent; and Chaplin, who was clerk of the peace for the county, also acted as his legal and political agent. So there is good reason to conclude that the whole affair was engineered.

'Dirty tricks' were all part of the electoral game, but on this occasion the sequel had momentous consequences for Aylesbury, for it enabled the Grenvilles and their supporters in the House of Commons to push through an Aylesbury Bribery Act in 1804, ostensibly to prevent any repetition of the 'notorious bribery and corruption' which had occurred in 1802. The Act extended the boundaries of the parliamentary borough to embrace the whole of the three hundreds of Aylesbury (about a fifth of the whole county), more than doubling the electorate to around 1,000 and so making large-scale bribery less feasible. Existing borough voters retained their existing household franchise for their lifetimes, while the new constituents were bound by the much less democratic 40-shilling freehold qualification used in elections for the two 'knights of the shire'. Aylesbury borough elections would never be the same again.

Even before the passage of the Aylesbury Bribery Act the Marquess was taking practical steps to extend his influence in the area, for in 1802 he purchased the whole of the Aylesbury manorial estate from the Pakingtons. He also purchased other properties in the town and he bought up sufficient unredeemed land tax in Aylesbury and Hartwell to create many new 40-shilling freeholders with votes in the newly enlarged parliamentary borough – more than fifty in Aylesbury alone. As a result the family was able for a time to share control of the representation of the two Aylesbury seats with the Cavendishes of Chesham, another Whig dynasty.

Then, in the general election of 1818, William Rickford staged a sudden coup by deserting his Grenville patrons and, backed by a wave of popular support, winning one of the two seats on his own account under the slogan 'May voters be Free and Representatives Independent'. He was the town's first resident MP since John Wilkes. More surprising still, the other successful candidate in 1818, who was none other than George Nugent-Grenville, Lord Nugent, of The Lilies, Weedon, near Aylesbury, younger son of the Marquess (as an Irish peer he could sit in the House of Commons), declared himself in favour of parliamentary reform. Since Rickford continued to represent Aylesbury in Parliament until 1841 and Nugent until 1832, the deep-laid schemes of the Marquess had produced very unexpected results.

The first four decades of the 19th century saw an unprecedented growth in the town's population from just over 3,000 in 1801 to 5,429 in 1841, an increase of 70.4 per cent, much of it the result of immigration from the surrounding countryside. This was a time of great hardship for labourers caused by unemployment and under-employment, exacerbated by the introduction of agricultural machinery locally and the rapid decline of the lace trade in the 1820s. Various expedients were adopted by the parish authorities to provide temporary relief for the unemployed, including the 'roundsman system' by which the men were sent round in gangs from one employer to another with the parish paying a proportion of the wages. At other times the whole responsibility of

91   *The Birmingham mail coach snowbound near Aylesbury in December 1836. The church spire is just visible in the centre distance,*

providing out-relief was farmed out to a contractor for periods of up to a year.

In 1829 it was decided to erect a new workhouse on a site near the Spittle mill on the Oxford road at an estimated cost of £3,000 and replace the existing premises in the churchyard area. It was decided, too, that in future single men and boys seeking work should be required to go into the workhouse or be allowed one shilling only in lieu of other relief. Soon afterwards Robert Nixon, a silk manufacturer from Manchester, approached the parish with an offer to promote a silk manufactory based on cheap pauper labour on the model of an existing factory at Tring. In 1833 the vestry undertook to modify a wing of the workhouse for use as a factory and to contribute to the cost of an extension, and in return for a lease Mr Nixon agreed to employ only the parish poor. Before long there were 40 looms in operation and the enterprise continued to flourish for many years. The new factory remained a benefit by itself, but hardly had the new workhouse been completed than responsibility for poor relief was taken out of the hands of the parish vestries by the New Poor Law Act of 1834 and vested in elected boards of guardians of newly formed poor law unions supervised by a central body of Poor Law Commissioners. Aylesbury thus became the centre of a union of 40 parishes or places and the eventual seat of a brand-new union workhouse.

Even more important for the future were the advances taking place in relation to transportation. In 1815, as the result of an initiative by several of its leading citizens, the town secured a 'cut', or arm, linking it at Marsworth to the main line of the Grand Junction (later Grand Union) canal, connecting the Thames at Brentford to the Oxford Canal at Braunston in Northamptonshire. The outcome was a 50 per cent drop in the price of coal locally and easier access to the London market for local livestock and agricultural produce, a great fillip to the economy of the town generally.

Twenty-one years later, in 1836, the London and Birmingham railway, the first ever trunk line to be constructed, arrived in the vicinity. Even before the main line was complete a move was on foot locally to provide a link from it to Aylesbury. A committee was formed; capital of £50,000 was raised by the sale of shares, locally and in London; an Act of Parliament was obtained, and by mid-1839 the Aylesbury-Cheddington line was completed, with a station originally located at Station Street, adjacent to the present High Street. It would be followed by other branch lines and stations before the arrival of the Metropolitan Railway finally provided a direct link to the capital in 1892. The promoters of the Cheddington railway included Thomas Tindal and his son Acton Tindal, another lawyer, William and Arthur Medley, Aylesbury bankers who went bankrupt in 1837, and two local landowners, George Carrington of Missenden Abbey and Sir Harry Verney of Claydon House near Winslow.

On completion, the line was leased to the London and Birmingham Railway Company, who provided the rolling stock. By 1840 the annual number of passengers was estimated at 32,000.

One unforeseen spin-off from the new rail link was the influx of wealthy visitors from the capital wishing to avail themselves of the sporting possibilities of the Vale, notably for hunting with hounds, made newly popular by the patronage of the Rothschild family, the international bankers who first began to settle in the area in the 1830s. It brought much trade and prestige to the larger local inns and in particular to the *White Hart*, whose colourful proprietor J.K. Fowler has left several entertaining volumes of memoirs containing many vivid glimpses of this aspect of the period.

Despite the competition, water-borne traffic continued to be important for the transport of heavy goods until well into the 20th century and the canal basin in Walton Street was for long a permanent home for a colony of boatmen, who even had their own floating chapel, as late as the 1920s. The effect of the railway on the coaching trade was, however, catastrophic and immediate. In 1841 John Gibbs, writing in the *Aylesbury News*, refers to James Wyatt, the celebrated Aylesbury coachman who had driven the *Dispatch*, the first coach to perform the journey to and from London in a single day, from 1816 until 1837, when in Gibbs's words 'the railway drove him from us'.

Seven

VICTORIAN AND EDWARDIAN AYLESBURY
(i) URBAN GROWTH AND
INDUSTRIAL DEVELOPMENT

The Great Reform Act of 1832 opened the way for a new era of far-reaching institutional and administrative change. As a county and district centre, Aylesbury benefited from many of the changes, both in employment opportunities and in public buildings. The new union workhouse (later the Tindal Hospital), built in 1844-5, was sited on the Bierton road on the outskirts of the town within sight of the new county gaol (now HM Young Offenders' Institute), erected at much the same time to replace the ancient, ill-designed premises behind County Hall. This in turn made room for a spacious Judges' Lodgings, completed

in 1850, a year after the return of the summer assizes to Aylesbury. Other new public buildings from this period included the County Lunatic Asylum (later St John's Hospital) built in rural surroundings at Stone, near Aylesbury, in 1850-3, and the County Constabulary Headquarters in Market Square in 1865 (the chief constable's imposing residence was just around the corner in Walton Street). In 1888 Aylesbury became the seat of the new Buckinghamshire County Council, but as yet without purpose-built offices.

Voluntary effort and philanthropy also played their part in the provision

92 *Aylesbury Union workhouse on the Bierton Road, built in 1844-5 under the Poor Law Reform Act replacing the former parish workhouse on the Oxford Road. It became the Tindal Hospital in the 1940s.*

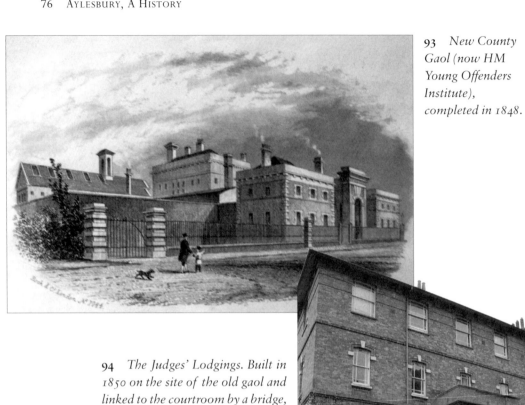

93   *New County Gaol (now HM Young Offenders Institute), completed in 1848.*

94   *The Judges' Lodgings. Built in 1850 on the site of the old gaol and linked to the courtroom by a bridge, it is invisible from Market Square.*

95   *The former County Asylum (St John's Hospital) at Stone, near Aylesbury, built in 1853.*

96   *New County Gaol: interior of cell.*

97   *New County Gaol: gallery.*

of public amenities, most notably in the case of the county infirmary, projected in the 1830s by Dr John Lee of Hartwell and rebuilt in 1859-62 with advice from Florence Nightingale to become the Royal Buckinghamshire Hospital (the building is now in private ownership) sited at the junction of the Buckingham and Bicester roads. It long remained a focus for charitable fund-raising.

By 1850 Aylesbury had acquired many of the characteristic attributes of a progressive Victorian town: a canal, a railway, a factory of sorts, gas street lighting provided by a gas company formed for that purpose in 1834 and local newspapers – sporadic in the 1820s, permanent from the 1830s – which circulated throughout the county. But it had also retained most of the problems associated with the worst forms of urban squalor, exacerbated by increased overcrowding. Although, as we have seen, the population grew by over 70 per cent between 1801 and 1841, there had been relatively little corresponding growth in the physical extent of the town. In the 10 years prior to 1841, for example, the total of inhabitants rose by 408, while the number of houses increased by a mere 75 (from 990 to 1,065) in the same period.

The result was a serious public health problem, especially in the poorer areas of the town. Expectation of life at birth was 28.25 years; infant mortality was proportionally high, with one in every seven children dying under one year of age; the death rate was 24 per thousand. The latter statistic was important because under the Health of Towns Act of 1848 the new General Board of Health was empowered, upon a petition showing a death rate of more than 23 per thousand, to hold a local enquiry. Aylesbury was one of the first towns to experience a public enquiry, held in December 1848, under the new Act.

Among the causes of mortality were found to be epidemic, endemic and contagious diseases. These diseases, which included an epidemic of cholera in 1832 in which 61 persons died, were chiefly found in the poorer districts, where houses were damp, ill-drained, ill-ventilated and lacking in water and sanitation. Among the places specifically mentioned in the official report were Whitehill, Spring Gardens (in Walton), Bierton Road, Dropshort, Walton near Bearbrook and Castle Street. There were also some 21 narrow courts and alleys, occupied by 700 people, with one or two privies at most in each court or alley, while no less than 19 courts and alleys were without any outlets. Sewage was emptied partly into the brook and partly into an open ditch. Existing sewers were mostly unusable. The poor obtained their supplies of water either from wells or from the brook, both sources mostly polluted. Dr Robert Ceely, 'district

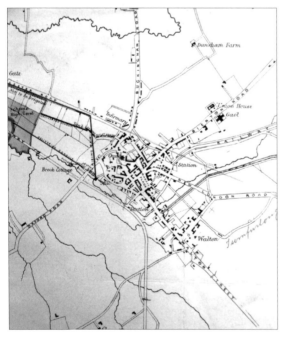

98   *Map of Aylesbury in the 1870s showing the abortive first piped water supply and sewage scheme on the west side of the town.*

medical attendant', declared bluntly in the local press that 'The state of the poor in this town is a disgrace to civilisation.'

The outcome of the enquiry was the creation of a Local Board of Health, elected by the ratepayers. This was not a temporary expedient. The new Aylesbury Board would be the principal organ of town government until it was replaced by an Urban District Council in 1895. The nine first members of the Aylesbury board were all men of substance. They comprised, in addition to Robert Gibbs, auctioneer, newspaper proprietor and future historian of Aylesbury, then aged 34, the following occupations: brewer, banker, wine merchant, grocer, landed proprietor (James Grace), farmer and two solicitors.

The comprehensive programme of sanitation envisaged in the 1849 report would occupy the new board and its successor body for most of the rest of the century, with many delays and wrong turnings. After several abortive schemes, the Chiltern Hills Spring Water Company was inaugurated in 1865 to supply the town with water, but in 1867 only a fifth of the town's houses had piped water laid on. Sewage works erected in 1870-1 on the west side of the town were found to be defective following a serious outbreak of diphtheria in 1885-6 and the £30,000 spent on new sewers was largely thrown away. Drainage, too, continued to present problems and Walton Street was frequently flooded in the 1870s and later. By 1911 the population of the town had reached 11,048, swollen after 1870 by the growth of industry.

Some development was already in progress in the town centre before 1849. An early impetus had been provided by the laying out of the New Road, the present High Street, in 1826. It was built to provide a more direct route for the Sparrowsherne

99   *Street scene, Kingsbury, late 19th century.*

100   *Ordnance Survey map of Aylesbury, surveyed in 1878-9, published 1884.*

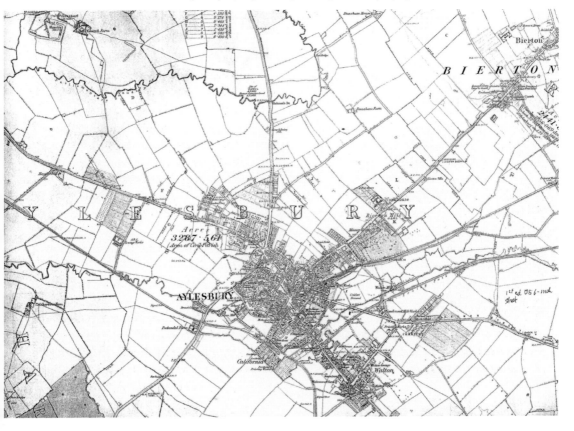

101 *Print showing Market Square, looking south towards the new Corn Exchange, late 19th century.*

turnpike (the A41), cutting through existing property boundaries, including parts of the extensive premises of the *George* and *Crown* inns in the process. By 1830 building lots were being offered for sale alongside two projected side roads, later to be known as Brittania Street and Railway Street. The two new streets would soon to be linked by Station Street (now the site of a multi-storey car park), the original location of the new railway station built in 1839. The High Street itself gradually filled up with buildings as frontage plots were sold. Many of the original buildings were substantial dwellings and some of the existing shops are later front ground-floor extensions. But by the 1880s High Street was on the way to becoming one of the town's principal shopping centres.

The financial collapse of the 2nd Duke of Buckingham and Chandos (1797-1861) in 1848, an event which shocked the nation, resulted in a series of sales of his extensive Aylesbury properties. The manorial rights as such were purchased by Acton Tindal, the Aylesbury solicitor and clerk of the peace for the county, who promptly built himself a large mansion on Bierton Hill, which he styled the Manor House. Sales of building plots soon followed. In 1853 Bull Close, site of the former Bull Farm (and previously of the *Bull* inn), the ancient manorial precinct, was put up for sale in 41 lots, mostly unoccupied, an area extending from the north-west side of Kingsbury as far as Whitehall Street on the west and from Buckingham Street south to the churchyard. Provision was made in the sale plan for two new streets, the present Ripon and Granville streets. However, progress in building was surprisingly slow, for the 1898 Ordnance Survey map shows that much of Granville Street was still empty of houses at that date.

The same seems to have been true of other building projects. One such scheme, launched in 1852, was the projected Northern Road estate off the Bicester Road, well outside the old urban centre. The building lease, to which Acton Tindal was a party, encompassed over 100 plots, but almost 30 years later relatively few plots not fronting the main road had been built upon. The 63 investors, mostly of up to three lots apiece, nearly all lived in Aylesbury and were mostly artisans. The area was eventually developed for industrial use. In contrast, higher-value middle-class houses, many of them three-storey villas, were being built piecemeal in Buckingham Street where a terrace of four handsome town houses (nos 61-7) bearing the date mark 1840 still survives near the present Coopers Yard car park, and also along the upper Buckingham and Bicester roads.

The arrival of the Great Western railway from Princes Risborough in 1863 produced some development on the west side of the town. Aylesbury now had two stations, both with only indirect links to the capital (a direct link had to wait until 1892). The new station (later known as the Aylesbury Joint Station) was situated on the edge of the former Friarage precinct, and as there was no existing road connection to the market place one had to be constructed. Great Western Street, of which little but the name now survives, was for long a busy commercial area. Adjacent to the station was a small grid-shaped development called California, laid out in building plots as early as 1849 – hence the name.

Large-scale development well beyond the existing limits began in the 1870s. It was most in evidence in the Tring Road area on the east side of the town, where the new industries of printing and milk-processing were sited, with major housing developments taking shape, first at Victoria Park and later at Queens Park. To the north, the Manor Park estate, begun in 1882, near the new prison on

102   *Route plan of the projected branch railway.*

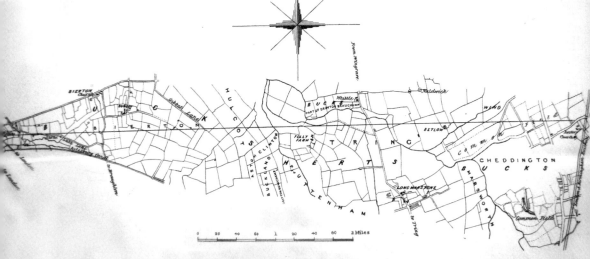

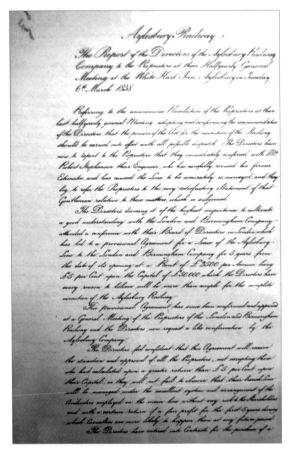

103   *Aylesbury Railway; Directors' Report, 1838.*

104a and b   *Aylesbury Railway Medal. It was struck to commemorate the opening of the branch line in 1839. Obverse shows portrait of George Carrington, Director, in profile.*

the Bierton Road was evidently aimed at more middle-class residents. By the 1890s, too, ribbon development was in progress in Walton Road beyond Walton village, an early example being the offer for sale by auction in 1895 of the *New Inn* together with 13 adjoining roadside plots (many of them subsequently subdivided) as sites for villa residences.

Despite these changes Aylesbury retained much of its market town character for the remainder of the century and beyond. The 1854 county directory describes it as 'quite an agricultural town ... having an excellent market once a week, which is well equipped with all kinds of grain, cattle, poultry, &c'.

Kingsbury is described as the chief market for cows and sheep. No fewer than six fairs are listed with two additional fairs, one in July for wool and the other in December for cattle. Agriculture had recovered from the depression years of the early decades of the century and would continue to flourish until the advent of cheap American grain in the early 1870s. Aylesbury itself still had 19 persons listed as farmers or graziers and three as cow keepers in 1851 and the census shows a considerable number of agricultural labourers, amounting to a surprising 10.5 per cent of the male population. The range of other occupations, as shown in an 1854 directory, did not differ radically from earlier in the century, but retailers and dealers – especially in food and drink and clothing – seem more numerous (42 hotels, inns and taverns and 23 beer retailers are listed). Some specialised services and crafts, such as coal dealers (11), cabinet makers and upholsterers (five), have expanded, and a few occupations (e.g. an accountant) are new to the town. Shoemakers (30) remain the most numerous of the craft workers.

Statistical analysis of the 1851 census returns confirms and refines these impressions. Craft industries, headed by shoemakers, tailors and brick makers,

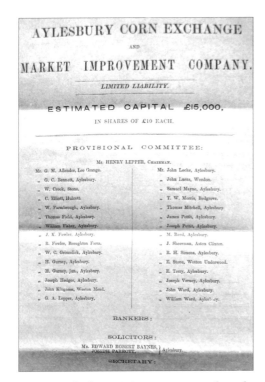

AYLESBURY CORN EXCHANGE

AND

MARKET IMPROVEMENT COMPANY.

LIMITED LIABILITY.

ESTIMATED CAPITAL £15,000,

IN SHARES OF £10 EACH.

PROVISIONAL COMMITTEE:

Mr. HENRY LEPPER, CHAIRMAN.

Mr. G. M. Allender, Lee Grange.	Mr. John Locke, Aylesbury.
„ G. C. Bennett, Aylesbury.	„ John Lucas, Weedon.
„ W. Crook, Stone.	„ Samuel Mayne, Aylesbury.
„ C. Elliott, Hulcott.	„ T. W. Morris, Bedgrove.
„ W. Farmbrough, Aylesbury.	„ Thomas Mitchell, Aylesbury.
„ Thomas Field, Aylesbury.	„ James Pettit, Aylesbury.
„ William Fisher, Aylesbury.	„ Joseph Pettit, Aylesbury.
„ J. K. Fowler, Aylesbury.	„ M. Reed, Aylesbury.
„ R. Fowler, Broughton Farm.	„ J. Sheerman, Aston Clinton.
„ W. C. Grimsdick, Aylesbury.	„ R. H. Simons, Aylesbury.
„ H. Gurney, Aylesbury.	„ R. Stone, Wotton Underwood.
„ H. Gurney, jun., Aylesbury.	„ R. Terry, Aylesbury.
„ Joseph Hedges, Aylesbury.	„ Joseph Verney, Aylesbury.
„ John Kingham, Weston Mead.	„ John Ward, Aylesbury.
„ G. A. Lepper, Aylesbury.	„ William Ward, Aylesbury.

BANKERS:

SOLICITORS:

Mr. EDWARD ROBERT BAYNES, } Aylesbury.
„ JOSEPH PARROTT,

SECRETARY:

105 *Prospectus of proposed Aylesbury Corn Exchange and Market Improvement Company, 1862. Its objectives included a covered market for meat, poultry, etc., and accommodation for livestock.*

of some 34 carriers. Also serving a wide area were the thirty-odd insurance agents listed, though these had other occupations in addition.

Thirty years later the new industries of printing and milk processing are represented in the 1881 census, where they already amount to 7.2 per cent and 1.4 per cent of males respectively, though in fact many of the milk factory workers were women. Retailers, at 16.7 per cent, were now the single largest group, followed by labourers (12.7 per cent), the building trades (12.3 per cent), agriculture (10.5 per cent) and craft industries (10 per cent). The marked decline in the position of craft industries was a widespread phenomenon at

accounted for 23.3 per cent of male employment. Next in succession come agricultural labourers and other 'primary workers' (17 per cent), retailing and dealing (12.6 per cent), building, etc., workers (11.9 per cent), professions and public services (7.4 per cent, in part reflecting Aylesbury's expanded county town status), domestic services (5.3 per cent) and transport (2.8 per cent). The census also reveals that Aylesbury had a far larger catchment area than any other town in the county, especially in retailing. It also had proportionately more lawyers, doctors, domestic servants and especially publicans (3.3 per cent) than the other Buckinghamshire towns. It is likely that at least some Aylesbury shopkeepers acted as wholesalers for country shopkeepers. Links with other local towns and the villages were maintained by a small army

106 *Formal opening of the Corn Exchange and Town Hall in October 1865.*

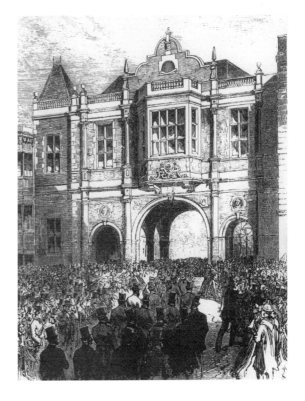

107 *Market Square from the south, late 19th century.*

the time and can be seen as a concomitant of the increase in retailing.

Local confidence in the town's market was demonstrated in 1862 with the launching of the Aylesbury Corn Exchange and Market Improvement Company with an estimated capital of £15,000. Plans included a covered market for 'meat, poultry, fish, fruit and vegetables, &c.', as well as improved accommodation for livestock. Corn exchanges were very much the fashion among market towns at the time, reflecting the expansion of the corn trade and the lack of space for holding livestock markets in town centres. The new Market Company brought about the removal of the old circular market house of 1808 in Market Square and the erection in 1865, at the south-east corner of Market Square at a cost of £27,000, of an imposing new Exchange building, a portion of which (the 'town arches') still stands. In order to make way for it, the

historic *White Hart* inn with its extensive premises was demolished. Facilities were also provided for a cattle market at the back of the premises. Unfortunately, the company soon fell victim to the depression of the corn trade after 1870. It was eventually purchased by the local authority in 1902 for £9,500. The livestock market continued to function and was in a fairly flourishing state in the 1890s with weekly sales averaging 470 sheep, 105 cattle and 215 pigs in 1896. The annual wool fair in July averaged 15,000 fleeces, compared to a reported 15-20,000 in mid-century.

One indigenous industry closely linked to agriculture was brewing. Aylesbury had four old-established breweries in the 1850s, but the only two of any size were John Dell's in Bourbon Street and Edward Terry's in Walton. Both had acquired chains of 20 or more 'tied' houses located over a wide area of the Vale and beyond. By 1864 Dell's brewery with its tied houses (there were 36 of them by 1872) had passed to Thomas and Joseph Parrott, the latter, an Aylesbury solicitor, having married Martha Dell. As Parrott, Walker and Co. they were taken over in the 1890s by the newly formed Aylesbury Brewery Company for £120,000. The Bourbon Street premises were demolished in 1894 to make way for public baths. The Terry family's Walton brewery company was also subsumed into the Aylesbury Brewery Company. Brewing in the town ceased in 1935 and the former brewery site near the canal in Walton Street has since been built upon.

The continued expansion of the town created opportunities for other local entrepreneurs. One craft industry of very long standing which expanded at this time was brick making, which was located on the east side of the town and was for a long time associated with the Read family. The 1854 directory lists two

brick and tile makers, Joseph Read and W.S. Locke and son. By 1891 the trade had been largely engrossed by a new firm, Webster and Cannon, who by this time were also builders on a very large scale, with a permanent labour force of around 500 men and a weekly wage bill of over £1,700. They gradually extended their activities, employing a team of skilled masons and specialising in churches and other large public buildings throughout southern England and the Midlands. The many local examples of their work include the Clock Tower (1876), Lloyds Bank (refacing, 1922) and the 'old' County Offices building (1929).

Not a great deal is known about the recent history of Aylesbury's two ancient watermills. Both seem to have been adversely affected by the loss of water consequent upon the construction of the canal. The Oxford Road mill was rebuilt

108   *Print of Hazell Watson and Viney's printing works in 1878.*

in the 1890s with supplementary steam power but finally ceased to operate in the 1920s. Walton mill had steam by 1843 and was described as a water and steam mill in 1879. It was acquired by Hill and Partridge, a local firm, around 1895, by which time it was grinding imported flour; it was still operating within recent memory.

A new phase in the town's industrial history began in 1867 when the London-based printers Watson and Hazell (Hazell, Watson and Viney from 1875) decided to open a branch in vacant premises in California. Lower property costs and a more salubrious environment were among the factors influencing the decision. The experiment proved a success and in 1878 a new and much larger factory was erected in the Tring Road close to the canal. By the 1880s the number of employees had risen to around four hundred. Many of the original work force had to be brought from London and elsewhere, but as time went on local boys were taken on as apprentices in increasing numbers. In contrast to the silk factory, the work was highly skilled and thus relatively well paid. The firm had a paternalistic attitude towards its employees and, in addition to good working conditions, provided a range of 'fringe benefits', including cheap housing and a works band.

Meanwhile, in 1870, the newly founded Aylesbury Condensed Milk Company had opened a factory, also situated on the Tring Road directly alongside the canal where, like Hazell's, it had its own wharf. Unlike Hazell's, this was a pioneering enterprise using a recently developed process to produce a new product of immense potential. As with Hazell's, the capital involved and the management were non-local, but the nature of the business was ideally suited to the area, for in Aylesbury's rural hinterland there was already a trend away from arable farming towards milk production for the metropolis. As a food processor the company contributed to the prosperity of the whole district. In the 1880s the factory was acquired by the Nestlé and Anglo-Swiss Condensed Milk Company, an early example of a multi-national business, with branches in Switzerland, Germany and the USA. By this time it was employing 150 workers, many of them female, and was processing 104,000 gallons of milk a month.

In subsequent decades both Nestlé's and Hazell's enlarged their premises, the latter more than once. In 1899 another printing firm, Hunt Barnard, opened in the Buckingham Road and in 1911 the Dominion Dairy started in Bicester Road. Both were medium-sized concerns. More important was the arrival of the curiously named Bifurcated and Tubular Rivet Company, usually shortened to 'Rivets', which built a factory at Stoke Road in 1910. By 1913 it was in the course of erecting many new houses for its workers. The Aylesbury directory for 1913-14 also lists the basket works of the LNER railway in Park Street, a new application of the traditional local craft of osier weaving, and Iris Cars Ltd in Mandeville Road. The railway also stimulated a revival of duck breeding – now largely based in the villages – for the London market.

Eight

VICTORIAN AND EDWARDIAN AYLESBURY
(II) POLITICS, RELIGION AND CULTURAL LIFE

After the Reform Act of 1832 politics in Aylesbury, as elsewhere, became more complex and less parochial. Whigs and Tories were gradually evolving into Conservatives and Liberals and mass political organisation played an increasing role. The 1804 enlargement of the borough constituency (now duplicated in the other county borough constituencies) meant that the parties were fairly evenly balanced. By 1840 the Conservatives had become the party of the farmers and the Church and the Liberals the party of choice for religious dissenters. Aylesbury even had its own branch of the Religious Freedom Society, of which Dr John Lee of Hartwell House, a man of strong liberal views, was a leading light.

The 1847 election was notable as the last in which Grenville influence played any part. Already in 1839 the 2nd Duke had been stripped of the lord lieutenancy of the county by the Whig government in favour of Lord Carrington of High Wycombe. Now a financial crisis deprived

the family of the bulk of their estates in the locality and thus of the political influence which still went with land and property. They were soon replaced by the Rothschilds, newcomers to the Vale, who gradually bought up former Grenville property through their confidential agent, the Aylesbury solicitor James James. Both as Jews and international bankers, the Rothschilds were natural Liberals and they formed an alliance which embraced both nonconformist, radical and middle-class townsmen and aristocratic Whigs such as

109 *Portrait print of Richard Plantaganet Grenville (1797-1861), 2nd Marquess of Chandos, afterwards (1839) 2nd Duke of Buckingham and Chandos, of Stowe near Buckingham, lord of the manor of Aylesbury. His extravagance was largely responsible for the spectacular collapse of the family fortunes in 1848.*

110   *Nathan Meyer Rothschild (1840-1915) of Tring Park, Herts., 1st Lord Rothschild (1885), MP for Aylesbury, 1865-85, Lord Lieutenant, 1889. He was the eldest of four Rothschild brothers who purchased estates in the area, attracted in part by a shared passion for hunting.*

111   *Recumbent Rothschild lion in Market Square, one of a pair presented in 1888.*

Carrington. The benefits were seen in the general election of 1852, when both Liberal candidates were elected.

In 1865 Nathan Mayer Rothschild (1840-1915), afterwards 1st Lord Rothschild of Tring Park, was elected as sole Liberal candidate alongside a Conservative and thereafter in successive Aylesbury elections between 1868 and 1880. In 1867 the second Reform Act, by establishing the male household franchise in the boroughs, extended the vote to working men thus, as far as Aylesbury town was concerned, broadly restoring the pre-1832 position, though it had the effect of tripling the borough electorate as a whole. Of even greater potential significance was the introduction of the secret ballot in 1872, though it did not make Aylesbury's working-class electors noticeably more assertive. The Conservatives even wooed the new voters by forming a local Working Men's Conservative Association, though its membership was not confined to manual workers.

Lord Rothschild's devotion to civil and religious liberty was genuine and his reputation for generosity did him no harm politically. The family's bounty was not confined merely to their endless donations and subscriptions to charities and good causes. They also left their mark on the town in the form of new buildings and facilities, including the former Literary Institute building in Temple Street, the Victoria Club in Kingsbury and public baths in Bourbon Street (since demolished). Yet it is the Conservative Disraeli, MP for the county from 1847 to 1876, and a frequent visitor to Aylesbury (he usually stayed at the former *George Hotel*), whose statue now stands in Market Square.

By 1881 the population of the parliamentary borough was just under 30,000 (9,000 of them in the town) with 4,403 registered voters. Under the third Reform

112   *The former Literary Institute in Temple Street, now a restaurant. Erected in 1879-80 by Sir N.M. Rothschild, Bt, MP, and extended northwards in 1903, it was one of many such Rothschild benefactions to the town.*

113   *Statue of Benjamin Disraeli (1804-81), Earl of Beaconsfield (1871), Conservative statesman and novelist, in Market Square, erected in 1914. He was MP for Buckinghamshire from 1847 to 1876 and was a frequent visitor to Aylesbury from his home in Hughenden.*

114   *Entrance to the Literary Institute showing the Rothschild monogram. The origins of the Institute can be traced back to 1819. It seems to have functioned for a period as the local Mechanics' Institute, a self-help society for working men.*

Act of 1884, which introduced household suffrage, and the accompanying Redistribution Act, the electoral district was expanded to form the single-member Mid-Buckinghamshire, or Aylesbury, division of the county, with a population of just under fifty-six thousand.

Throughout this period organised religion was playing an increasing part in a great many aspects of social life, much of it through voluntary action, and was gradually helping to create an ethos of greater 'respectability'. The national census of religious worship of March 1851 showed an aggregate recorded attendance of 5,151 at all Sunday services, of whom 2,542 – stated to be an estimate only – were Anglicans (total population 6,081). Allowing for multiple attendances, this suggests that a fairly high proportion of the estimated 70 per cent of the population (i.e. 3,256) who were able to attend actually did so.

By the 1840s efforts to reform the Established Church, both institutionally and spiritually, were having effects locally. In 1845 as a result of legislative action the archdeaconry of Buckingham was transferred from the huge diocese of Lincoln, to which it had belonged since the Conquest, to the neighbouring diocese of Oxford. The Bishop of Oxford, Samuel Wilberforce (1805-73), was a leading reformer who was determined to improve the tone of church life and to provide resident clergy and church schools in every parish.

On his death, aged 80, in 1842 John Morley had been succeeded by the Rev. J.R. Pretyman, MA (1815-99). The new vicar was a member of a wealthy clerical dynasty and his father had been the last prebendary of Aylesbury. In 1844 he married one of the daughters of Thomas Tindal, the lawyer, soon to be lord of the manor. The 1851 census shows that he and his young family were cared for by a manservant and three female servants. Pretyman's appointment coincided with the creation of the new district church of Holy Trinity, Walton. Projected in 1838 by public subscription, it was the result of a breakaway movement by the Low Church section of St Mary's who thought that the services there were becoming too High. The building was consecrated in 1845, with an extension in 1849. Under the Rev. W. Pennefather, who was its inspirational vicar from 1848 to 1853, and who initiated a mission to the local bargees, for whom he provided a floating chapel, Walton acquired a reputation for hostility to ritualism.

Pretyman later developed conscientious scruples over Church doctrine which led him to resign the benefice in 1853 when still under forty. It was during his time that the decision was finally taken to restore the parish church, as its condition was such that restoration, long postponed, could no longer be put off. The parish vestry still had the legal right to raise a compulsory rate on parishioners of all religious persuasions for this purpose, but there was resistance from the nonconformists. Mr Pretyman contributed to the debate by publishing a pamphlet defending church rates on scriptural grounds. In the event a crisis was averted and the parishioners agreed to borrow £3,000 on the rates to enable the work to proceed (by 1850 the rate had been paid by 1,030 people) and a further £2,000 was raised by public subscription.

Under the direction of George Gilbert Scott work on the interior of the church was largely completed between 1849 and 1855 (services were resumed at Whitsun 1851), in the course of which all the old box pews and galleries were ejected. A second phase, lasting from 1866 to 1869, dealt with the exterior. The individual

115 *The Rev. Edward Bickersteth, D.D. (1814-92) was vicar of Aylesbury from 1853 to 1875 and was also archdeacon of Buckingham. A distinguished churchman, Archdeacon Bickersteth acquired a national reputation in the 1860s as a spokesman for the clergy in Convocation. This caricature appeared in Vanity Fair in 1884 when he was dean of Lichfield.*

116 *Catalogue of books in the Aylesbury Circulating Library, 1840. Founded in 1819, the library had a stock of 742 books. It cost four guineas to join and there was an annual subscription of four guineas, so membership was effectively confined to the better off.*

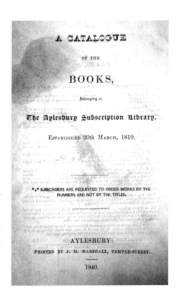

stained-glass windows were paid for by prominent local families, notably the Tindals, who gave the great west window, and the Rickfords and their relations. The new seating, funded mainly by subscription, provided 1,020 places, 251 more than before. They included 521 free and children's seats; previously there had been only 55 free seats.

Mr Pretyman's successor was Edward Bickersteth, DD (1814-92), who was vicar from 1853 until 1875. He was also archdeacon of Buckingham. A distinguished churchman, he became a national figure in 1860 as the prolocutor, or speaker, of the lower house of the revived Convocation of Canterbury. As vicar he promoted church schools and found a site for St John's district church in Cambridge Street (since demolished), which opened in 1881. During his time an increasingly active parish life developed. Organised activities, good works and good causes abounded and these included excursions and other leisure activities. By 1870 the level of literacy among the population generally was acknowledged by the introduction of a parish magazine combining improving reading, supplied by an outside source, with inserts of parish news.

Bickersteth was followed by Arthur P. Purey-Cust, DD (1875-6), who began building the present vicarage, and Arthur T. Lloyd, 1876-82, 'a most powerful and eloquent preacher'. J.K. Fowler, local worthy, author and staunch churchman, says of Bickersteth and his two successors that 'the parochial reign for more than thirty years of three such men has had a great and beneficial effect on the character of the people... not only in the town, but in the whole neighbourhood'. The net annual value of the living is given in 1894 as 'about £300', which seems distinctly modest for a town such as Aylesbury. Yet by 1891, besides the vicar, there were four unmarried curates who also served St John's church. They shared a communal existence in a 'clergy house' adjacent to the vicarage.

On the evidence of the one-off 1851 census of worship the largest nonconformist congregation was still the Independents/ Congregationalists, with 767 attenders. They included in their ranks many of the town's most prominent and prosperous

117 *Steeplechase organised by J.K. Fowler, the sporting proprietor of the* White Hart, *over his own land at Prebendal Farm in 1847. Horse racing did not displace hunting to hounds, the sport traditionally associated with the Vale of Aylesbury: the hunt was still meeting in Market Square in the 1920s.*

citizens, notably the families of Gibbs, Rolls and Payne. Their church at Hale Leys was rebuilt in 1874 and although later demolished its tower still stands in the High Street. Next in order of size were the Wesleyan Methodists at 700 (an estimated figure), the Primitive Methodists (394) and the Baptists (358). The present Methodist church in Buckingham Street, built in 1893, was the last major nonconformist church to be built. Also listed were the (Roman) Catholics (130, of which 100 were evening attendances) and a group styled simply 'Christian' (20-30), who met 'to worship God alone and private'. The Catholic chapel (in the new High Street) is stated to have been 'very lately opened'.

Like the Anglicans, the nonconformist churches sponsored social and charitable societies and organisations of their own. In 1894, for example, the Congregational church had a congregational guild (founded 1889) whose objects were 'mutual friendship, mental culture, spiritual development, recreation and co-operation in doing good'. In addition there were a mothers' meeting and associated self-help society

and coal club, a clothing society of 50 years standing, and a sick visitors' society embracing all the nonconformist churches in the town and dispensing help 'irrespective of any religious distinction'.

Education was a field which had earlier been considered outside the direct purview of the state, to be provided by voluntary endeavour, if at all. So the beginning, in a small way, of government grants-in-aid for elementary education in 1833 gave a fillip to the founding of new schools for the poor and intensified the rivalry between Anglicans, most of whom favoured the National Society, which sponsored Church schools, and nonconformists, who supported the rival, non-denominational, British and Foreign Society. In Aylesbury such rivalry was muted before 1840 as Mr Morley, the then vicar, was a warm supporter of the British School erected in Pebble Lane in

118   *The Italianate Methodist church in Buckingham Street, erected 1893-4.*

1830. The existing Free Grammar School was an independent charitable foundation without any religious test for admission, but the (head)masters were invariably in holy orders and pupils were taught the church catechism. In 1843 59 boys out of 100 were nonconformists. In the 1830s the British School was forced to close its doors for lack of funds, leaving only the Grammar School and a number of small commercial establishments (some of them boarding schools), of which 10 are listed in an 1842 directory.

The situation was altered in 1839 when a new archidiaconal board of education was established, with committees in each deanery, in order 'to promote, improve and extend popular education according to Anglican principles'. It aimed to obtain trained teachers, to inspect their work regularly and to try to bring other schools into union. The board was able, on the sale of the old parish workhouse premises in Oxford Road in 1842, to acquire some of the land as the site for a National School (later St Mary's Church of England School). By 1847 there were 70 day pupils, including 22 girls. A further 148 children (boys and girls) attended Sunday school only. In 1849 National Schools were erected in Walton to serve the newly created district parish. Before this, in 1842, the British School had reopened, following a meeting of subscribers attended by Dr Lee of Hartwell and Lord Nugent, a past and future Liberal MP for Aylesbury. Thus by mid-century there were, apart from the Grammar School, three elementary schools in the town which were accessible to the poorest children: the British School, which was for boys only, and the two National Schools, which also took in girls.

The condition of the Grammar School at this time was far from satisfactory. The number of staff had been reduced from

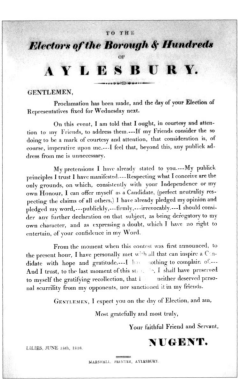

119 *Election address by Lord Nugent (1789-1850), younger son of the 1st Marquess of Buckingham (he inherited his title from his Irish mother), 1818. A radical in politics, he was several times elected as one of Aylesbury's two MPs.*

three to two in defiance of the rules and attendance had dropped to well below the permitted number. Matters came to a head in 1849, when a public meeting was held and an address forwarded to the trustees. Complaints included unsatisfactory attainments; the imposition of charges for instruction and materials; boys forced to perform menial tasks; and lack of progression from the English to the Latin department. An examination held by a government inspector in early 1850 confirmed that many of the boys could scarcely read and that their attainments were 'far below those of scholars in the National and British schools'. When the trustees proved recalcitrant it was decided to petition the Lord Chancellor for a remedy. The upshot was a new scheme of management and a thoroughgoing reform of the rules which laid down *inter alia* that poor boys aged at least seven, able to read, should be eligible for admission to the lower school absolutely free and that at least ten places in the Latin School should be reserved for boys who had attended the English department.

With the Education Act of 1870 the state took upon itself for the first time the responsibility of ensuring that every child in the land should have the chance to attend a proper school staffed by proper teachers (attendance was soon made compulsory and, by 1891, free). The Act provided that new school boards should be established in all districts where the existing provision was deemed insufficient. Because religious teaching in them was to be non-denominational, the school boards were unwelcome to many Church people and as a result there was a frantic outburst of school building in many places, to avert the need for a board, as well as bitter wrangling between Anglicans and nonconformists.

In Aylesbury matters were managed more amicably than elsewhere, for decisions were taken both to enlarge St Mary's National School in 1870 and also to rebuild and enlarge the British School, which had been condemned as substandard by the government inspector, and a mutual approach was made to the trustees of Harding's charity for assistance with the necessary funding. Grants of £700 each were forthcoming and smaller grants were also made to the Church schools in Walton and in Cambridge Street, but this new and questionable use for the ancient apprenticing charity did not entirely escape criticism. The average aggregate attendance at all four schools was over a thousand.

The state of education in the town in the 1890s still left much to be desired, in the opinion of at least one observer, though the elementary schools were judged 'fairly efficient', on the evidence of their examination results. But change was in the air following the transfer of responsibility for both primary and secondary education to the county councils in 1889. Under the new regime progress was soon made towards realising some of the desired improvements. The British School was closed in 1907 and its pupils transferred to newly built premises in Queens Park off the Tring road (now the Queens Park Centre), where new working-class houses were going up, and the same year saw the transfer of the Grammar School (now to be a mixed school) to its present premises in nearby Walton Road. The mixed aspect did not find favour with everyone. Co-education ceased with the opening of a separate high school for girls, also in Walton Road, in 1959.

Nine
NEW BEGINNINGS: 1910-2000

The reign of George V began amid the looming threat of war with Germany. Since Aylesbury was the headquarters of the Oxfordshire and Buckinghamshire Light infantry, its inhabitants must have been more aware of the danger than most and their fears can hardly have been allayed by the holding of extensive military manoeuvres in the county during 1913 and earlier. A large number of Aylesbury men volunteered for service, including many from the Hazell works. The war memorial erected in Market Square in 1921 bears no fewer than 264 names of the fallen. In 1914 the Southern Works factory was built in Bicester road for the manufacture of bell tents for the army, of which 1,400 were produced in 1914 alone. This wartime industry disappeared with the return of peace, but the premises remained and were later used by a succession of enterprises. Aylesbury Grammar School was pressed into use as a military hospital for at least part of the war. Soldiers' wives, left behind, had to cope as best as they could. In other ways, presumably, life went on much as it had always done. The industry most affected by war appears to have been brewing, which suffered from official restrictions on the supply of grain.

While the war was still in progress Aylesbury became a municipal borough under a royal charter granted in 1917. Strangely, the formal petition which preceded the grant makes absolutely no reference to the war or to any resulting diminution of trade. It begins by referring to the loss of the 1554 charter and points out that Aylesbury was, with one exception (Oakham in Rutland), the only county town in England which was not already a municipal borough, this despite being the seat of the county assizes and quarter sessions and the headquarters of the County Council. It goes on to list the town's many other features which made it a worthy candidate for incorporation. The public buildings cited include, in addition to the County Hall, the 'fine county Museum' maintained by the Buckinghamshire Archaeological Society, a state female convict prison and inebriate reformatory (the former county gaol), the recently enlarged Royal Buckinghamshire Hospital with accommodation for 85 patients, 'a large and commodious' town hall and municipal buildings partly used as a corn exchange, assembly rooms and a covered butchers' market.

Economically, too, the picture painted in the petition is, while perhaps over-rosy, one of prosperity and progress. The evidence cited includes the 'rapid' increase in size and population in recent years (from just under 8,000 in 1881 to just over 11,000 in 1911); the 'much frequented' market which, it is claimed, attracts buyers of stock from London and other large towns, the tolls of which, together with rents from the town hall, bring in a revenue of £500 to £600 yearly; and the printing works and other new industries, employing over 1,500 hands between them. The town is also said to be an important shopping centre, cheap market tickets being issued by the various railway companies on market days and largely made use of in the surrounding neighbourhood. Not mentioned, but also significant, was the network of carriers that still connected the town (mostly twice-weekly) to some 45 villages and towns round about, extending as far as Oxford, Bicester, Berkhamsted, Chesham, Watford and Uxbridge.

Other recent advances mentioned are the complete system of sewerage constructed on modern lines; public lighting by gas, intended soon to be replaced by electricity from the town's mains, which would also provide cheap power to the 'numerous factories and workshops in the town'; a water supply provided by a company

based in the town; and 'exceptionally favourable' railway branch lines, which now included a direct link to London via the Metropolitan line extension, opened in 1892.

Cultural and social amenities were not forgotten. There were 10 places of worship including the medieval parish church, a recently rehoused co-educational grammar school and elementary schools as well as social and working men's clubs and two newspapers. Public works included public baths, allotments, an isolation hospital and a steam fire engine, four banks and a number of excellent hotels. The area of the town within its existing boundaries is given as 3,301 acres, i.e. approximately the same as that of the ancient parish, and the number of dwellings as 2,822.

The first mayor, alderman R.W. Locke, who had served on the UDC since its inception, was a brick manufacturer and coal merchant. He appears to have been fairly typical of his fellow councillors and many of his successors in office were also to be drawn from a commercial background. Perhaps the most colourful holder of the office in the inter-war period was Giacomo Gargini (1935-8), proprietor of the *Bull's*

120   *(Left) Medal commemorating the unveiling of Aylesbury's war memorial in 1920.*
121a and b   *Aylesbury Bread Show, 1909. Silver medal awarded to A.J. Burch. According to a local directory for 1913, he kept the Golden Grain Bakery in Stoke Road and was awarded many other medals for his bread.*

Head hotel in Market Square and responsible for its mock-medieval re-fronting.

After the war the new corporation soon found itself directly involved for the first time in the construction of new dwellings as a result of legislation in 1919 designed primarily for the replacement of sub-standard housing by 'homes fit for heroes', as the current slogan had it. Between 1920 and 1929 some 400 high-quality low-density municipal houses were built in the new Southcourt housing estate on the former Prebendal farm on low-lying ground on the west of the town – the first significant expansion of the town on that side – on land purchased from the Church Commissioners. The tenants were provided in large part by slum clearance, carried out in White Hill and vicinity, Chapel Row (opposite the canal basin), Anchor Lane and Prospect Place in Walton (opposite Holy Trinity church) and other now largely forgotten corners of the old town. Some of the insanitary cottages thus disposed of were several centuries old. Hazell, Watson and Viney had made their own contribution to the housing supply by building houses near their printing works for the use of their employees in 1895. Further additions to Southcourt were made at intervals between 1929 and 1940, as a result of which the estate almost doubled in size.

In contrast, there seem to have been relatively few large-scale post-war private housing developments before the 1930s, which saw the building of the Abbey Road estate on the Bicester Road and renewed building in the Tring Road area, mostly on the south side at Walton Way, Fairmile and Regent Road. There was also development at Manor Drive in Manor Park on the Bierton Road. Much of the population growth mentioned in the charter petition had in fact occurred between 1901 (9,099) and 1911 (11,048); thereafter growth in

122 *Brochure for the* Old Bull's Head *in Market Square, demolished in 1964.*

fact remained comparatively low until after 1931, by which date the population had reached 13,387.

A picture postcard printed around 1910 had proudly proclaimed that 'It [Aylesbury] easily takes its place among the market towns of England, the supplies of agricultural dairy produce to London being immense.' Most of the produce had been exported by rail. By the 1920s, however, the Aylesbury duck trade, said to have produced some quarter of a million ducks a year, mostly destined for the capital, at the height of its fame, was again in decline, largely owing to disease and the high cost of duck food. Improved communications had also facilitated the spread of outside influences on country towns all over Britain. In Aylesbury the first of the chain stores had made an appearance by 1908, when

This double page: 'Old Aylesbury' in the early 20th century: photographs from a survey of historical monuments made c.1911. (All seven are Crown copyright)

123   (Left) The former Rising Sun *public house in Oxford Road.*

124   *Temple Square is Aylesbury's smallest square and the least altered. This photograph shows the south-east side.*

125   *Temple Square, north-west side. Church Street is on the right.*

126   *Temple Street, north side. The building on the corner was demolished in 1974.*

127   *(Below) Temple Street, south side. The building with the tall chimney is the Literary Institute.*

128   *(Above) The 17th-century former* Forester's Arms *public house in Church Row (now Pebble Lane).*

129   *Walton Grange (16th-century) in Walton Road, the Hazell family residence. It was destroyed by a land mine in World War II.*

130 *A notice of film programme, 1913, for the Market Theatre. The supporting feature had a strong local interest. The bride was the daughter of the vicar of Aylesbury, the Rev. C.O. Phipps, and the groom was the adopted heir of Sir Arthur Liberty (d. 1917), founder of the great London store. The reception was held at the Prebendal House, the bridegroom's residence.*

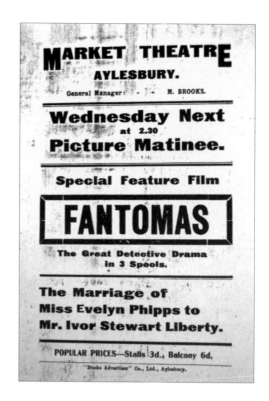

a branch of Boots the Chemists opened in Market Square (now the Halifax building) and there was a fish and chip shop in the town in 1913. Longley's in the High Street was the town's first department store, though a home-grown one. In 1914 the new Aylesbury Market Theatre, run by the Aylesbury Electric Theatre Company Ltd, was showing 'high class varieties and star pictures' twice nightly. Opened in 1911 and seating 650, it was one of the earliest purpose-built cinemas in the county. The introduction of tarmac surfaces to the county's roads by the County Council in the 1920s made motoring popular locally and led to the replacement of carriers' waggons by regular motor coach services. A new age was dawning.

The new industries referred to in the charter petition continued to provide employment and even – at least in the case of Hazell, Watson and Viney and Hunt Barnard, the printers – to expand. The old-established Aylesbury Brewery Company, however, ceased to brew beer in 1937. That there was also an increase in employment in administration is evident from the erection in 1929 of the 'Old' County Offices, a 17-bay block in brick and stone located in Walton Street, conveniently close to the town hall and corporation offices and later to the County Police Headquarters

131 *Directory advertisement for Hawkins' motor and motor cycle garage, 1913.*

132   *Tinted postcard view of the north-east corner of Market Square showing a cattle sale in progress c.1900. The entrances to the High Street and Cambridge Street can be seen in the background. Lloyd's Bank is just out of sight on the left of the picture.*

133   *Line-drawing of machine room at Hazell, Watson and Viney's printing works, 1939.*

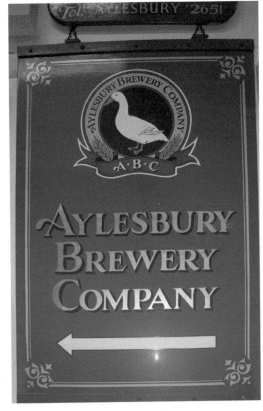

134   *Business plate for the Aylesbury Brewery Company.*

135   *The Anglo-Swiss Condensed Milk Co./Nestlé's factory on the High Street in 1908 by Nick Carter.*

in Exchange Street, built in 1935. Both the latter were the work of local builders Webster and Cannon. Despite all these changes Aylesbury between the wars still retained a good deal of its former rural atmosphere, though less so after the sale of cattle in the square was completely discontinued in 1927. Some Aylesburians can still remember the sound of hammer on anvil ringing out from the smithy in Walton street and the sight of animal blood oozing from beneath the door of a slaughter house in the town centre.

Given its size and geographical situation it is hardly surprising that the impact of the Second World War on Aylesbury was not particularly dramatic, but as elsewhere in the county the surface calm could be deceptive. The RAF already had a base at nearby Halton, but a new airfield was set up a little to the north of the town at Wescott in Waddesdon parish to train bomber pilots, one of a network of such airfields hidden away in the countryside. After the war it became a top-secret rocket research establishment with a staff of up to

1,800, many of whom lived in Aylesbury. The Czech government in exile was lodged at the nearby village of Wingrave. Secret experiments on special weapons were carried out at The Firs at Whitchurch ('Winston Churchill's Toy Workshop') for which Roblin's, the Aylesbury engineers, supplied some of the devices. The Rivets Company manufactured the special rivets used in the wings of all Spitfire and Lancaster warplanes. In 1943 the first penicillin production factory in the country was

136   *Business plate for the Nestlé and Anglo-Swiss Condensed Milk Company. It ceased trading in 2002.*

137   *The Hazell, Watson and Viney premises on the Tring road shortly before demolition in 1982.*

established in a part of the Nestlé's factory in High Street; here under the direction of the Glaxo company large quantities of the life-saving drug were prepared for the D-Day landings with the help of local labour. It was the imminent threat of war, too, which was responsible for the building of an emergency hospital at Walton, now known as Stoke Mandeville Hospital and world-famous for its pioneering paraplegic unit associated with the name of Ludwig Guttman and for its part in the birth of the Paralympic Games.

More prosaically, as in the previous conflict, strategic industries such as International Alloys moved to the town to escape the bombs and the accompanying staff were housed in 'pre-fabs'. Wartime work was also carried on again in the Bicester Road factories. Agriculture once more became important – and profitable – under the direction of the War Agricultural Committee. Yet the only enemy bomb of consequence dropped on the town was a landmine which so severely damaged the Hazell family residence, Walton Grange,

in Walton Road (now the site of the High School) that it had to be demolished.

Even before the war had ended, plans were being made for the town's future expansion. When they finally came to the point of implementation in the early 1960s it was in the context of the post-war legislation for the relief of congestion in the major cities and the prevention of urban sprawl associated with the New Towns movement. One alternative to the New Town as such was the controlled expansion of selected existing towns. This meant obvious economies for all the parties concerned, but it also had the disadvantage of making extensive redevelopment for road widening, car parks, etc., inevitable. In 1959 Aylesbury entered into a formal agreement with the London County Council under which it became an 'overspill' town for the reception of both people and industry from the capital in return for grant-aided provision of new infrastructure, amenities and financial assistance towards house building. The quota of new dwellings agreed for occupation by families moving from London was fixed at

3,700, of which fewer than 1,000 remained to be completed in March 1981 when it was estimated that a further 4,600 new homes would be required by 1991, including around 1,800 for which planning permission had already been granted.

A comprehensive scheme for the zoning of future land use under the agreement was embodied in the Aylesbury Town Map, approved in 1961, which envisaged a population of 42,000 by 1974. Already in 1971, by which date Aylesbury had been identified by government as one of six 'medium-growth areas' within the region, the figure had reached just over 40,500, an increase of 12,500 on 1961 and approaching twice the total growth in the previous decade. In contrast, a new and more spectacular experiment under the provisions of the 1952 Act was being launched in north Buckinghamshire in 1971 with the acceptance of the master plan for the new city of Milton Keynes, envisaged as a 'regional complex' incorporating several existing towns and villages.

In Aylesbury redevelopment within the ancient town centre in the 1960s followed the lines of an existing plan drawn up locally as early as 1950. It was concentrated in the south-west side of Market Square and the area immediately adjacent, including Great Western Street, old Friarage Road and the south side of Walton Street, leaving the rest of the historic core area largely intact. But though limited in its extent, the redevelopment proved controversial. Many local people regretted the complete demolition of the historic Silver Street with its quaint, if dilapidated, 'period' buildings, the product of centuries of 'infilling', and the massive complex of new structures which replaced it was far from universally popular.

Most controversial of all was the new County Offices in Walton Street,

138 *Lloyd's Bank, Market Square, erected 1853, is in the direct line of succession to the 'Old Bank', founded by William Rickford and his father in 1795.*

opened in October 1966, the 12-storey concrete- and granite-faced tower which dominated its surroundings, dwarfing the 18th-century brick-built County Hall and symbolising the arrival of a new era in the town's history. It was linked at mezzanine level across Great Western Street (above a cavernous bus station) to the new Friars Square shopping centre. This was a brick and concrete complex on several levels fronting Market Square; completed in 1967, it incorporated an open-air market area into which stallholders were moved from the square. The new market, which was used as the setting of a scene in the futuristic film *A Clockwork Orange*, proved decidedly unpopular and was converted in 1991-2 into the present Cloisters area of Friars Square, a sort of indoor market area with a separate entrance at lower ground level from Great Western Street. After this the market traders were allowed to return to the Market Square. A later redevelopment of the early 1980s on the other side of Market Square was the Hale Leys Centre, a relatively inconspicuous shopping mall linking to the High Street,

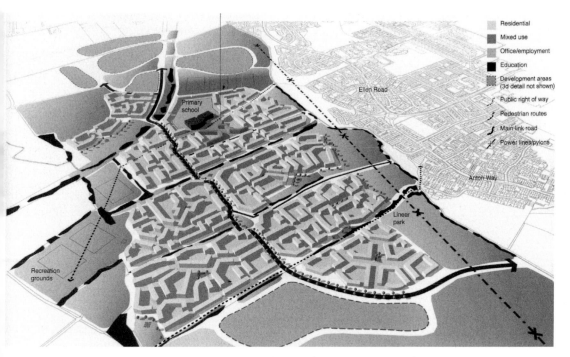

139a *Aylesbury will continue to expand in the future and the map shows shaded areas to the south-west, south and east where development could take place.*

139b *Proposed development on the periphery of Aylesbury will take the form of self-contained villages with all amenities.*

142   Walton Street also has striking examples of modern commercial architecture, notably the so-called 'Blue Leanie' (shown here on the left), built as offices for The Equitable Life Assurance Society in c.1982, and the ESRI UK offices directly opposite.

140   This stylish block of flats is at Old Brewery Close, fronting Walton Street.

141   The town centre seen from the top of the County Offices in Walton Street, looking north-east. In the foreground fronting Walton Street is the neo-Georgian Old County Offices (1928-29 and 1939). Exchange Street is visible on the right.

143   *(Left) The canal basin at Walton Street. In the background are the County Offices and the new theatre under construction and in the foreground a 19th-century warehouse.*

144   *The town centre seen from the top of the 12-storey County Offices tower block (1963-6) in Walton Street, looking north-west. In the centre left is the clock tower in Market Square and at the bottom are the roofs of buildings fronting Walton Street with, beyond, the backs of County Hall and other buildings in Market Square. Friars Square, the 1980s shopping centre, is front left.*

145   *Erected in 1963-66, the tower block of the new County Offices building in Walton Street is still Aylesbury's only high-rise building and is a landmark for miles around.*

146   *Church Street, south side. The building on the left is The Chantry, once the home of Aylesbury's pioneer historian, Robert Gibbs (d. 1892) The tall chimneys on the extreme right belong to cottages rebuilt for Hickman's Charity in 1871. Hickman's now provides accommodation for some 90 alms people in addition many other good works.*

the front entrance to which was on the site of the former *Bull's Head* inn, with side access from Exchange Street via a multi-storey car park.

Work was also proceeding on the projected ring road. Apart from the new, partly re-aligned, Friarage Road linking Walton Street and Whitehall Street/ Oxford Road, this was based on existing routes, but it involved enormous disruption and the destruction of a great many houses and other buildings, the majority of them modest structures of Victorian or later date. Despite all this effort, it was several decades before the ring road was finally completed. More recently a five-lane central road 'hub' has been put in place to provide for a town public transport network.

By 1981 Aylesbury's historic core was almost surrounded by modern housing of various kinds. Following the precedent set by the Southcourt estate, local authority housing was mostly located on the west side of the town and private developments on the east, though this pattern became gradually less consistent over time. The largest privately built housing development, the Bedgrove estate, was begun as early as September 1959 and was completed in July 1973. It comprised a total of 1,723 homes on a 300-acre site and was at the time the largest housing estate in the kingdom. Between 1961 and 1978 owner-occupied housing increased from 37.9 per cent to 47 per cent, while private rented and other accommodation declined from 25.6 per cent to 10.8 per cent in the same period. Of later private estates Watermead, with its artificial lake and mock period houses, is the most distinctive.

More recently approved developments have been on the fringe of the ancient parish, including Fairford Leys (formerly Coldharbour Farm), which comes close

147   *The canal at Willowbrook Terrace. On the left is the metal footbridge which gives its name to the late 19th-century Highbridge Walk.*

148 *The Civic Centre (1974-5). Unimposing architecturally, but highly functional for public events, its impending demise will be regretted by many. It is concealed from view behind the Corn Exchange.*

to the historic Hartwell House and its landscaped grounds, and latterly Berryfields on the edge of the scheduled ancient monument site at Quarrendon (3,000 new houses approved in 2006) and Weedon Hill. An application to build 1,600 houses on ecologically important meadow ground at Broughton-Stocklake, between the disused railway line and the canal, was turned down in 2004, thus preserving an important green 'lung' extending into the town centre. But canal-side apartment blocks have been erected on the former Nestlé site in Park Street and are increasingly appearing on, or near, the ring road.

The day-to-day needs of the new residential areas are served by small groups of three or four local shops, typically including a grocer and a newsagent. A few estates, notably Bedgrove on the southeast edge of the town and Walton Court on the west, were more fully provided for. Jansel Square in Bedgrove has a parade of 16 shops and is able to attract customers from outside its immediate area, while the Walton Court centre incorporates a supermarket and seven other shops, with other community facilities. In contrast, the Fairford Leys estate off the Oxford road, a late arrival, though provided with numerous community facilities (including a church and school), is limited to a pharmacy, presumably because it has easy access to the town centre shops.

Availability of employment was a key element in the town's growth. During the early 1960s the first of the new manufacturing firms relocated to the town, usually bringing up to 40 per cent of their workforce with them, thus giving a boost to factory employment locally. They were mostly sited on new, modern, industrial estates located outside the town centre in Gatehouse Road, Bicester Road, Stocklake and elsewhere. Growth was comparatively rapid at first, but there was a slow-down in manufacturing after 1965. Many of the town's growth industries, particularly in

149 *Apartment blocks have been a feature of recent town-centre property development. This one, typical of many, is built on the site of the former Nestlé factory and backs on to the canal.*

150 *Artist's impression of the new canal-side theatre and shopping centre in Exchange Street, near the canal basin, scheduled to open in 2010.*

printing and electronics, were affected by automation with consequent negative effects on employment requirements.

The mid-1960s to early 1970s saw a second phase of industrial development, with a large increase in employment in service industries, reflecting in part an increase in demand sparked by earlier growth, but also the arrival of major national service organisations, for which Aylesbury had attractions as a location for office development. In 1971 the percentage figures for employment in manufacturing and in service/construction respectively were 35.7 per cent and 64.3 per cent; in 1977 the equivalent figures were 30.4 per cent and 69.6 per cent. The number of jobs increased by about 7,700 in this period. In 1977 the old-established printing industry was still the largest source of manufacturing employment, with just under 2,000 employees, followed by electrical engineering (1,785) and mechanical engineering (1,611), while the largest two service sectors were professional and scientific (7,739, reflecting in part the expansion of local administration) and the distributive trades (4,935).

The period after 1980 saw the gradual disappearance of Aylesbury's older-established industries. Hazell, Watson and Viney did not long survive a takeover by the Robert Maxwell publishing empire; most of the site is now occupied by a Tesco superstore. Rivets closed in 2000 and was redeveloped for housing. Nestlé's was last to go, closing in 2002; the buildings were later torn down to make way for apartment blocks. Today Aylesbury's economy is dominated by services, including financial services. One financial giant, Equitable Life, has since been forced to cease trading. Its former offices in Walton Street, popularly known from its distinctive design

as 'The Blue Leanie', has been joined by other modern office and apartment blocks, some of them of architectural merit, in the same street.

The original intention of the planners was to concentrate shopping facilities serving the town, and to a lesser extent its catchment area (estimated at some 8-10 miles radius), in the town centre. Supermarket chains were already on the scene in the 1960s and were expanding nationwide, resulting in fewer and larger shops. In Aylesbury there had originally been a strong presumption against permitting edge-of-town or out-of-town shopping centres, but this proved impossible to sustain in the longer term as the demand for more large stores increased. By the 1990s Aylesbury was ringed around with supermarkets and superstores set alongside outsize car parks, most of which were situated close to the ring road or to other major routes. 'Discount warehouse' trading, on the other hand, was tolerated on some of the new industrial estates almost from the start. It was later directed to the former brickworks site in Cambridge Street, now refurbished and extended as the attractively designed Junction Retail Park, and to a number of other locations deemed suitable.

The first decade of the new century has seen the launch of a new phase of development in the town centre with the start of work on the controversial Waterside project on the south side of Exchange Street, which will include a 1,200-seater new theatre and shopping facilities. Planners now predict that the town's population will reach 100,000 over the next quarter century. Meanwhile, in 2006 Aylesbury Vale district was briefly in the top 10 of an independent 'quality of life' league table, scoring 77.1 for employment and 75.7 for owner-occupation.

SELECT BIBLIOGRAPHY

Adair, John, *John Hampden*, 1976

Beckett, John, *The Rise and Fall of the Grenvilles, Dukes of Buckingham and Chandos, 1710-1921*, 1994

Bernard, B.W., *The King's Reformation*, 2005

Blair, John, *The Church in Anglo-Saxon England*, 2005

Boatwright, Lesley (ed.), *The Buckinghamshire Eyre of 1286*, Bucks Record Soc., Vol. 34, 2006

Brandwood, Geoff, 'Aylesbury Church and its Restoration by George Gilbert Scott', *Records of Buckinghamshire (Records)*, 34, 1992

Broad, John and Hoyle, Richard (eds), *Bernwood: The Life and Afterlife of a Forest*, 1997

Buckinghamshire Record Society publications (edited editions of, and indexes to, selected historical texts relating to Buckinghamshire)

Carswell, John, *The Old Cause: Three Biographical Studies in Whiggism* (Thomas Wharton, pp.27-119), 1954

Cash, Arthur H., *John Wilkes*, 2000

Chenevix Trench, John and Fenley, Pauline, 'The County Museum Buildings, Church Street, Aylesbury', *Records*, 33, 1991

Cheshire, C.J., 'The Growth of Aylesbury and the Development of its Urban Morphology, 1878-1937' (unpublished MA thesis, 1958, in CBS)

Chitty, A., *Advisory Development Plan for Aylesbury*, 1950

Cockman, F. G, 'The Railways of Buckinghamshire' (unpublished typescript in CBS), 1971

Crouch, David, *William Marshall*, (2nd ed.), 2002

Crouch, Col. Guy, 'The Building of County Hall', *Records*, XII, 1927-33 (supplement)

Dalton, R. and Hamer, S.H., *The Provincial Coinage of the 18th Century* (part 1), 1910 (booklet, illustrated)

Davis, R.W., *Political Change and Continuity 1760-1885: a Buckinghamshire Study*, 1972

Dell, Alan, *William Rickford, MP (1768-1854)*, 1986

Durham, Brian, 'Traces of a Late Saxon Church at St Mary's, Aylesbury', *Records*, XX, 1978

Elvey, Elizabeth, 'Aylesbury in the Fifteenth Century. A Bailiff's Notebook.', *Records*, XVII, 1965

Farley, Michael, 'Burials in Aylesbury and the Early History of the Town', *Records*, XXI, 1979

Farley, Michael and others, 'A Late Iron Age and Roman Site at Walton Court, Aylesbury', *Records*, XXIII, 1981

Fowler, J.K., *Echoes of Old County Life*, 1892

Fowler, J.K., *Recollections of Old Country Life*, 1894

Fowler, J.K., *Records of Old Times*, 1898

Gibbs, Robert, *A History of Aylesbury*, 1885 (reprinted 1971)

Gibbs, Robert, *Buckinghamshire. A Record of Local Occurrences, 1400-1880*, 1878

Hagerty, R.P., 'St Osyth and St Edith of Aylesbury', *Records* XXIX, 1987

Hampton MSS (Pakington estate records). Microfilms in CBS.

Hohler, Christopher, 'St Osyth and Aylesbury', *Records*, XVIII, 1966

Hanley, H.A., *The Prebendal, Aylesbury: A History*,1986

Hanley, H.A., *Thomas Hickman's Charity: A Tercentenary History*, 2000

Hanley, H.A., 'The First Century of Bedford's Charity, Aylesbury, 1494-1597', *Records*, Vol. 35 for 1993

Hanley, H.A., *Apprenticing in a Market Town: The Story of William Harding's Charity*, 2005

Hepple, Leslie W. and Doggett, Alison M., *The Chilterns*, 1992

Hunt, Bettridge and Toplis, *Index to Probate Records in the Archdeaconry Court of Buckingham 1483-1660 & Peculiars 1420-1660*, Bucks. Record Soc. Vol. 32, 2001

Jenkins, J.G., *Calendar of the Roll of the Justices on Eyre, 1227*, Bucks Record Soc., Vol. 6, 1942

Keefe, H.J., *A Century in Print: the Story of Hazells 1839-1939*, 1939

Kessler, David, *The Rothschilds and Disraeli in Buckinghamshire: An Essay*, 1996

Le Hardy, William (ed.), *Buckinghamshire Sessions Records* (calendar), 1678-1733, with addenda 1663-1720, 1953-7, 1980

Linehan, Lawrence, 'The Bishop and the Editor'[The *Bucks Free Press*], *Records* 34, 1992

Linehan, Lawrence, 'The *Bucks Herald*, Its Politics, Supporters and Finances, 1832-1867', *Records* 40, 2000

Lipscomb, George, *History and Antiquities of the County of Buckingham* (4 vols), 1847

Lloyd Hart, V.E., *John Wilkes and the Foundling Hospital at Aylesbury, 1759-1768*, 1983

Manton, J. and Hollis, Edwin, *Buckinghamshire Trade Tokens Issued in the Seventeenth Century*, 1933 (illustrated)

Mead, W.R, *Aylesbury Grammar School 1598-1998, a Commemorative Volume*, 1998

Morris, John (ed.), *Domesday Book: Buckinghamshire*, 1978

Page, William (ed.), *Victoria History of Buckinghamshire* (4 vols), 1904 (reprinted 1967)

Parker, J., 'The Manor of Aylesbury' (with text of court roll, 1499-1500) in *Archaeologia*, 1885

Parrott, Hayward, *Aylesbury Town Yesterdays*, 1982

Pevsner, N. and Williamson, W., *The Buildings of England: Buckinghamshire*, 2nd ed., 1994

Priest, St John, *General View of the Agriculture of Buckinghamshire*, 1813

Reader, Francis W., 'Tudor Mural Paintings in the Lesser Houses in Bucks', in *Records* XII, 1927-33

Reed, Michael, *The Buckinghamshire Landscape*, 1979

Rowley, Trevor, *The English Landscape in the Twentieth Century*, 2006

Royal Commission on Historical Monuments (England), *An Inventory of the Historical Monuments in Buckinghamshire*, vol. 1, HMSO, 1912

Sheahan, J.J., *History and Topography of Buckinghamshire*, 1861

Stenton, F.M., *Anglo-Saxon England*, 2nd ed., 1946

Thorpe, David, *Buckinghamshire in 1851: The Evidence of the Population Census*, Bucks Arch. Soc. Papers No. 2, 2002

Viney, Elliott and Nightingale, Pamela, *Old Aylesbury*, 1976 (revised 1977)

Waters, A. and others, *The Kings Head, Aylesbury: an Historic Buildings Survey*, The National Trust, 1993

INDEX

Note: Page numbers in *italics* refer to illustrations and captions